6-19-74

KENYA
*The Politics of Participation
and Control*

Written under the auspices of the Center
of International Studies, Princeton University, and
the Center of International Affairs, Harvard University.

A list of other publications of the
Center of International Studies and a list of
other books on Africa written under the auspices of
Harvard Center for International Affairs
appear at the back of this book.

KENYA

The Politics of Participation and Control

BY
HENRY BIENEN

PRINCETON UNIVERSITY PRESS
PRINCETON, NEW JERSEY

L.C. Card No. 73-2461
ISBN: 0-691-03096-0

Library of Congress Cataloging in Publication data
will be found on the last printed page of this book.

This book has been composed in Linotype Times Roman

Printed in the United States of America
by Princeton University Press

1807596

For Laura, Claire, and Leslie

Acknowledgments

Much of the published work on Kenya has concentrated on the colonial period. Among the growing body of material and analysis on independent Kenya a good deal is still unpublished. I am grateful to the scholars who have been kind enough to let me see their work over the last years. Thanks are due to Bruce Berman, Goran Hyden, Peter Hall, Jay Hakes, Frank Holmquist, John Harris, Raymond Hopkins, Colin Leys, Apollo Njonjo, Richard Sandbrook, Marc Ross, John Okumu, Michael Todaro, Susan Mueller Tufte. Many of them went way beyond the call of duty in sharing their work. Sidney Verba and Ken Prewitt made available interesting studies of political participation before publication.

I spent 1971-72 as a periodic and commuting fellow at the Harvard Center of International Affairs. My colleagues commented on my work and made available their own case studies and analytical frameworks. I am especially grateful to Samuel Huntington and Joan Nelson for providing the stimulus and encouragement to think about Kenya in the context of general concern with problems of political participation. Joan Nelson made detailed and valuable comments on the draft of this manuscript. Gary Wasserman of Columbia University showed me his interesting work on Kenya and made helpful comments on the manuscript too.

I owe thanks to a number of institutions who helped my work along. I was able to go to Kenya in 1968-69 through the generosity of the Rockefeller Foundation and Princeton University. R. Kirby Davidson of the Rockefeller Foundation was most helpful at all times.

Acknowledgments

The Center of International Studies at Princeton supported me both before and after the field-work in Kenya through secretarial and financial assistance. I owe Cyril Black, Director of CIS, thanks for his assistance. I owe a special debt to the staff of CIS. Over the last years I have greatly benefited from the always efficient and friendly help of Jane McDowall, June Traube, Mary Merrick, Joanne Weissman, and Dorothy Dey. They have deciphered the undecipherable and met impossible deadlines. They have my greatest appreciation. I also received support from Princeton's Woodrow Wilson School of Public and International Affairs for the summer of 1971 which enabled me to work on Kenyan materials.

The University of Nairobi provided me with a physical and intellectual home during 1968-69. There were many Kenyans who took time from busy schedules to meet with me. Two in particular continued our association and friendship back in Princeton: Bildad Kaggia, head of the Maize Marketing Board, and Robert Ouko, Minister for East African Affairs. I am grateful to the provincial commissioners and district commissioners, and the provincial and district trade and planning officers who met with me. I am also grateful to the officials in the President's Office and other Ministers who provided time and information.

I am deeply appreciative of the editorial assistance of Mrs. Polly Hanford of Princeton University Press.

My thanks to my wife, Leigh, are always great.

Henry Bienen

November 1972
Ibadan, Nigeria

viii

Contents

List of Tables

KENYA
*The Politics of Participation
and Control*

Abbreviations

AFC	Agricultural Finance Corporation
APP	African Peoples Party
ICDC	Industrial and Commercial Development Corporation
IDS	Institute for Development Studies
KADU	Kenya African Democratic Union
KANU	Kenya African National Union
KAU	Kenya African Union
KPU	Kenya Peoples Union
TANU	Tanganyika African National Union

I

Introduction: Kenya and the Problem of Political Participation

Kenya has been a country of great interest to students of African politics. Kenya and the Ivory Coast together have been to some observers signal "success stories" after independence. Kenya, like the Ivory Coast, has had more than a respectable rate of growth in gross domestic product. Both countries have had neighbors to contrast them to. *Ghana and the Ivory Coast* is already the title of a book.[1] *Kenya and Tanzania* is sure to follow and the comparisons between the two East African countries are many.[2] And both Kenya and the Ivory Coast have opted for seemingly clear strategies of economic growth based on a determination to keep ties to western countries and gain foreign aid and investment; both have concentrated on growth rather than redistribution. Both countries have been controlled by a "maximum leader" and a small

[1] Philip Foster and Aristide Zolberg, eds., *Ghana and the Ivory Coast* (Chicago and London: University of Chicago Press, 1971).

[2] See for example, Goran Hyden and Colin Leys, "Elections and Politics in Single-Party Systems: The Case of Kenya and Tanzania," Nairobi, 1971, unpublished paper. Also, A. W. Seidman, "Comparative Development Strategies in East Africa," *East Africa Journal*, Vol. 7, No. 4 (April 1970), pp. 13-18. Reginald Green wins the prize for hitting three out of four in his "Four African Development Plans: Ghana, Kenya, Nigeria, and Tanzania," *Journal of Modern African Studies*, Vol. 3, No. 2 (1965), pp. 253-274.

group around him who have strong ethnic ties with each other. Indeed, both countries could be characterized by an attitude among the ruling group of "benevolent elitism."[3] Some observers would say that the elitism is not so benevolent. Indeed, if Kenya and the Ivory Coast have been put forward as countries on the road to economic development and political stability through the pragmatic leadership of their founding fathers, they have also been picked out as symbols for all that has been wrong with African patterns of development since the end of formal colonial rule. They are seen to be countries where neo-colonial influence is strong and where a parasitical elite of top politicians and civil servants squeeze the rural areas for their ill-gotten gains. They are seen to be without ideology, a sin in the eyes of those for whom the absence of a leader's writings in anthologies on socialism in developing countries or "ideologies of the Third World" is equated with the absence of any conception of development or even national interest and dignity or sense of nationhood.

In Kenya's case, the national movement has been said to have been betrayed. The sense of bitterness among Kenya's critics is the greater because Kenya had such a traumatic colonial past. Africans fought and died during Mau Mau only to have the loyalists and the Europeans win out in the end, it is argued. It is said that the African elite has accepted the norms of the old rulers. The critics of Kenya point to a faction-ridden party, the

[3] This term was applied to Kenya by Marc Howard Ross, "Grassroots in the City: Political Participation and Alienation in Nairobi After Independence," unpublished manuscript (Bryn Mawr, Pa.), 1971, p. 304.

Kenya African National Union (KANU), which remains an empty shell. They maintain that power resides in a small clique around President Kenyatta and is wielded through a Civil Service which is colonial in form and substance, down to its very pith helmets. Growth takes place at the expense of the poor: the rich get richer and the poor stagnate or worse. A privileged elite distributes the benefits of economic growth that it gains through alliances with Europeans and through expropriation of Africans and Asians to tribal clients unfettered by any of the formal mechanisms of control which reside in the Legislature and elections. In the process, it exacerbates tribal tensions and creates them where they did not exist before. This same elite arrogates to itself the wisdom to choose a path for development on the grounds that people do not understand developmental problems and will, if left to themselves, allocate resources on a short-run calculation for schools, clinics, roads, and other immediate benefits. Curtailing effective mass participation is thus justified. Organized dissent is not allowed and the heavy hand of civil administration and, if need be, police and riot squads are used to put down opposition. All this from the critics.

In the face of an economy which has grown at better than 6½ percent per annum between 1964 and 1970, the critics insist that Kenya's strategies are at dead end. Unemployment is pointed to; the growing problem of secondary and primary school-leavers is underlined. Rapid rates of urbanization are noted as is the expanding population in the rural areas. What institutions, it is asked, can handle these problems? What strategies will this kind of elite develop which can deal with the structural problems? Kenya's growth, it is argued, is hostage

5

to foreign investment, aid, and other external items like tourism.[4] The pros and cons of the argument are interesting in their own right and for what they may tell us about possibilities for the future in Africa. But the arguments are hard to get hold of decisively. For one thing, data on income distribution or corruption or even unemployment is not easy to come by or necessarily reliable when it is available. Moreover, Kenya as a case study of African problems of development is complicated by a number of things. It had a major land reform program in the 1960s which itself built on earlier land registration and consolidation and which has remained highly controversial. It

[4] Kenya's critics have been numerous. A major assault is Oginga Odinga's *Not Yet Uhuru* (New York: Hill and Wang, 1967). Another is the unpublished autobiography of Bildad Kaggia. Among the scholarly community, economic analyses which stress Kenya's failure to deal with structural problems and the inheritances of the colonial system are Seidman, "Comparative Development," and A. W. Seidman, "Comparative Industrial Strategies in East Africa," *East Africa Journal*, Vol. 7, No. 6 (June 1970), pp. 18-42; A. W. Seidman, "The Dual Economies of East Africa," *East Africa Journal*, Vol. 7, No. 5 (May 1970), pp. 6-19; Jacob Oser, *Promoting Economic Development* (Nairobi: East African Publishing House, 1967); Green, *op.cit.* For political analyses see John Okumu, "Charisma and Politics in Kenya," *East Africa Journal*, Vol. 5, No. 2 (February 1968), pp. 9-16; Ahmed Mohiddin "Sessional Paper No. 10 Revisited," *East Africa Journal*, Vol. 6, No. 3 (March 1969), pp. 7-16. Critics of Kenya's party and representative institutions have been many. See Raymond Hopkins, "The Kenyan Legislature: Political Functions and Citizen Perceptions," prepared for Shambaugh Conference on Legislative Systems in Developing Countries, University of Iowa, November 11-13, 1971. One of the most interesting social structural arguments is Colin Leys, "Politics in Kenya: The Development of Peasant Society," *British Journal of Political Science*, Vol. 1, No. 3 (1971), pp. 307-337.

is early to assess that land reform. The bitter colonial legacy and the salience of a particular tribal group, the Kikuyu, has marked independence politics. Party politics and the patterns of factionalism have been influenced by the fact that Kenya's ruler is an old man, *Mzee* Kenyatta, whose own style and role have been elusive to outside observers.

There are more general problems, which pertain to forming and operationalizing concepts.

If we eschew the term development itself and use a different nomenclature to ask questions like: Is Kenya a representative society? Or, how participant is Kenya? Or, what is the weight of class and ethnicity in Kenya politics? we still run into problems as to what we mean in these instances. We can have no decent measures of participation, or class, or for that matter economic development until we decide what it is we are talking about. Development economists may argue that per capita income and gross domestic product figures alone should not measure economic development and that employment and income distribution ought to be added in. Once it is agreed to do that, the measures can still be precise.[5] Any discussion of how representative a ruling group is of society or how participant the society is involves thorny problems as to the way society is conceived and an understanding of who the ruling group is.[6] We can, of

---

[5] Operationalizing the concept "welfare," however, can be as thorny as operationalizing the concept "representation."

[6] Of course, it is not easy to measure how Government taxes and spends and how individuals and groups benefit or lose from the extractions and allocations of Government. A recent study which tries to assess the impact of Government taxing and spending in Kenya is John R. Nellis, *Who Pays Taxes in Kenya?*, Research Report No. 11, Scandinavian Institute of African Studies, Uppsala, 1972.

course, *define* a particular concept clearly and use a definition consistently but at the same time miss what may be important in the process we hope to analyze, using our definition as a point of departure. Take the attempt to understand political participation as an example of difficulties both in conceptualization and data collection. The issues surrounding political participation in the political science literature are not synonymous with all the concerns which fill the debate between the critics of the Kenyan way to development and those who see Kenya's example as a practical alternative under conditions of great constraint on leaders. The notion of political participation does, however, speak to many of the core issues in this debate. How elitist is Kenya? Who gets what, and when, and how? What do party and faction mean in Kenya and what are the consequences of party patterns and the importance of the Civil Service and individual leadership? Can all these ad hoc questions be subsumed under generalized questions of political participation?

Political participation has become a grab-bag concept in much the same way that political development became in the early 1960s. Just as studies titled "The Political Development of . . ." were often political histories of a particular country, so there now abound studies called "Political Participation in . . ." which are often descriptions and sometimes analyses of government and politics in a general way. At the same time, other efforts are devoted to defining political participation, just as much time and effort were spent in elaborating definitions of political development. Indeed, definitional distinctions have been even more involved in the literature on political participation since participation is often thought to be as much an attitudinal phenomenon as a structural and behavioral one. Many studies of political participation have come to be studies of all the politics of a society when participation has been understood in the broadest possible manner. At panels and colloquia on participation where most of the time has been spent trying to delimit the subject matter under discussion, the cry has gone out: What is not participation?

Why then has political participation become an organizing concept for so much contemporary work in developing countries? One reason probably has to do with available tools of analysis. Scholars interested in developing countries have been increasingly using techniques developed in the study of American and West European politics. Samples of populations in Third World countries can be surveyed to find out their attitudes about and activities in politics. The concerns as well as the techniques of the pioneering study *The Civic Culture*[7] seemed obviously relevant to the politics of developing countries. What did citizens expect of the state? What was the locus of their loyalties? The very newness and weakness of many states gave added interest to these questions. If, as Almond and Verba put it, the heart of democracy had to do with citizen competence and participation, could not the politics of new states, the gap between state and society, be understood as a problem of political participation?

It was clear to observers that when new states were created out of colonial territories, nations did not necessarily spring into being. Much of the literature of the 1960s analyzed the problems of nation-building. Karl Deutsch and his students analyzed processes of social mobilization and the creation of new patterns of social

[7] Gabriel Almond and Sidney Verba, *The Civic Culture* (Boston: Little, Brown, 1963).

9

interaction and political participation.[8] Deutsch called attention to the expansion of politically relevant strata, those who had to be taken into account, as parochial loyalties broke down and social mobilization occurred. New social and economic patterns generated new political pressures, it was argued. In a similar vein, the Social Science Research Council's group on political development referred to crises of legitimacy, integration, and participation which did not appear sequentially in the Third World but came all at once.[9]

Political participation remained center stage in the work of Samuel Huntington. He called attention to the dangers of increasing participation under conditions of weak institutions which obtained in Asia, Africa, the Middle East, and Latin America.[10] Huntington's explicit concern was for stability. Increased participation meant expansion of effective demands in societies where demands could not be accommodated easily. He, like many other scholars, stressed the short-run destabilizing effect of increased political participation. By the late 1960s, the early association of participation with democracy had given way to this concern for stability.

Perhaps, out of our awareness of and concern for the weakness of institutions in developing countries, we are

[8] For an early and influential statement see Karl Deutsch, "Social Mobilization and Political Development," *American Political Science Review*, Vol. 55 (September 1961), pp. 439-514.

[9] See Myron Weiner and Joseph LaPalombara, eds., *Political Parties and Political Development* (Princeton: Princeton University Press, 1966), and especially pp. 13-42. Also see Lucian Pye and Sidney Verba, eds., *Political Culture and Political Development* (Princeton: Princeton University Press, 1965).

[10] Samuel P. Huntington, "Political Development and Political Decay," *World Politics*, Vol. 17, No. 3 (1965), pp. 386-430.

relatively neglecting the nature of support for regimes. Certainly, we must keep analytically distinct political participation and political demands. We want to look at the relationship between them, not to define the concepts contingently. It may be that if certain demands are met or anticipated by a political leadership, certain kinds of political participation can be foreclosed. People may get what they want with relatively low levels of participation. It is also true that many ruling groups are very narrowly based and continue to exist because they are irrelevant to the lives of most of the people they ostensibly rule while they can coerce the relatively few groups that would contend with them. There are other countries where Government is in touch with its people in many ways: through services provided, taxes extracted, controls imposed on political life, and opportunities opened for participation over new issues or in new ways or in new arenas. Kenya is such a country.

An examination of participation and control in Kenya may be useful for calling attention to the aspects of participation which pertain to support for a regime and not merely to their destabilizing effects. Kenya also shows that leaderships have alternatives in the kinds of participation they try to encourage and curtail and that they can make choices in the arenas for participation which they try to provide or withhold. It is necessary to be explicit about what is meant by participation.

I do not want to review once again the literature which concerns itself with how we best can conceptualize political participation but I must do this a bit since there is a problem about what we mean by participation. We cannot measure increases in participation without having a definition which makes sense. Discussions of the definitional problem have often centered on the following

11

questions: Does political participation have to do with shared political activity? If individual participation ought to count, should we also be examining activities not necessarily designed to influence anyone; that is, ought we to look at noninstrumental, expressive activity? By political participation do we mean political activities that do influence others' conduct in fact? What about failed attempts to do so? Are we referring to capacities for action or only actual behaviors? Are we to concentrate on forms of participation, e.g., institutional action, direct or indirect, violent or nonviolent? Are we going to turn the problem around and ask a contextually rooted question such as: What do the people concerned consider most important? What are their own definitions of participation? Do these change over time? Or does participation matter? That is, if people get what they want, do they care about whether or not they can trace their own influence to any output?

It does not suffice to recognize that these questions exist and then say: we can only measure voting or have crude measures of interest-group activity so we will call these phenomena political participation. It would be better to simply call them voting behavior and interest-group activity. Indeed, political participation may itself be so broad a notion that unless we break it up we have nothing much at all. Even if we take behaviors rather than attitudes as the defining elements of political participation, if political participation refers to the behaviors of individuals designed to affect either directly or indirectly the outcome of political decisions in their society, we are in a very broad realm indeed.[11] And when partici-

[11] Marc Howard Ross, relying on Lester Milbrath's *Political Participation* (Chicago: Rand McNally, 1962), defines participation this way in "Urbanization and Political Participation: The

pation is used to refer to the incorporation of more and more of the population into modern forms of economic and social activity we run the risk of obliterating all meaning.[12] It may be that commercialization of agriculture, shift of labor into industry, rural and urban migration are critical processes going on in a society and that they have important political consequences. But to call them political participation is to eschew any hope of looking at relationships between social, economic, and political phenomena.

Sidney Verba and his colleagues exclude psychological orientations like efficacy as measures of participation and also exclude activities like "following politics" or discussing politics with one's neighbors because they have in mind a core definition of participation as the means by which interests, desires, and demands of the ordinary citizen are communicated with a view to more or less directly influencing the selection of government personnel and/or the decisions they take.[13] Yet these notions raise

---

Effect of Increasing Scale in Nairobi," unpublished paper presented at the Annual Meetings of the African Studies Association, Boston, October 21-26, 1970, p. 8. Earlier in the same paper Ross says, "Political Participation means engaging in activities through secondary as well as through primary based ties" (p. 3). This notion emphasizes the shared action aspects of participation.

[12] "Notes on Participation in Modernizing Societies," prepared for the discussion of the Colloquium on Political Participation, Harvard University, Center for International Affairs, 1971.

[13] Sidney Verba, Norman H. Nie, and Jae-on Kim, *The Modes of Democratic Participation: A Cross National Comparison*, a Sage Professional Paper. Series No. 01-013, Vol. 2, Beverly Hills, 1971, p. 8. For a similar treatment see Irma Adelman and Cynthia Taft Morris, "A Conceptualization and Analysis of Political Participation in Underdeveloped Countries," Part II, Final Report, to Agency for International Development (AID),

difficulties as to how direct is "more or less" direct. Verba wants to exclude acts that manifest symbolic support for government as acts of participation but such symbolic acts may be translated into influence at some later date. And what of citizens who want to avoid being acted on but who do not initiate action to influence? The argument can be made that peasant politics is often the politics of avoidance of government edict without much sense on the part of the participants that they can affect Government policy in the future by some present act. Thus the actors may spend most of their effort insulating themselves from Government or removing themselves from Government's reach.

It is also one-sided to focus on the participation of ordinary citizens when the actions of elites are such a critical aspect of participation. We want to know what dimensions of participation and modes of participation count for different layers of the population, different ethnic and economic groups, for actors in different institutional settings.

Verba et al. call our attention to the idea that political participation should be thought of as a multidimensional rather than a unitary phenomenon. And Ross argues also persuasively for Nairobi that participation is not unidimensional but rather that there has been an independence style cluster of patterns for participation and a post-independence style cluster. The most important areas of political participation in the struggle for independence were attendance at rallies, voting, joining a party, paying party dues, working for a candidate. These are all

Grant IDCsd-2236, February 1971. Adelman and Morris write of "voluntary activities" but degrees of voluntariness are critical and we could not easily dichotomize all political acts as voluntary and involuntary.

14

activities related to elections. The second style is not related to elections or to the mobilization efforts of the political elite but shows a pattern of activity in which the population seeks to acquire information and present its views and demands to the elite.[14] Activities like following the news, talking politics, making contact with higher placed persons defined this pattern. Not surprisingly, social status was related differently to the two patterns as were ethnic factors, feelings of estrangement, organizational variables.[15]

If one had gone back to an even earlier period of Kenyan history, the period of the Emergency or Mau Mau during the 1950s, one would have found yet other dimensions of participation, including violent ones, of course. We shall return to these matters. Here it is necessary to point out that if non-elites can be differentiated by modes and styles of participation, so can elites both among themselves and as compared to non-elites.

Difficulties arise if we focus only or even largely on individual and group attempts to influence Government or highly placed individuals. Groups try also to directly influence each other or to eliminate others from an arena. Sometimes this elimination is a physical one. We can go so far as to say that much of politics in developing countries takes place as groups deal with each other without Government as an intermediary. Sometimes this is the politics of ethnic violence; sometimes it is the politics of ethnic alliances. Factional groupings come and go at times without reference to Government or semipublic authorities like parties, trade unions, and associational groups.

We can start with Verba's notion of participation as

[14] Ross, "Urbanization and Participation," pp. 9-11.
[15] *Ibid., passim.*

15

an attempt to influence Government by individuals and groups, but add concern for groups' and individuals' attempts to influence each other directly on issues which become public issues or have the potential to become public issues.[16] Private land transactions can become public issues if they threaten to disrupt public order. Private agreements among groups not to bring forth certain issues into the public arena ought not to be excluded from examination. We should also be concerned with acts of Government officials and those who try to mobilize parts of the population from above. If we leave these aspects of politics out, do we gain more than we lose?

Patterns of institutional development and group formation cannot be understood by an exclusive focus on the attempts of social, political, and economic groups to communicate with Government and influence it. Institutional development and group formation must also be understood as a process molded by elites. Government's attempt to structure this process is only one attempt by elites to do this. Further, it makes no sense to look at the ways that individuals participate in politics without considering the nature of social and economic groups, cleavage, and institutions in society.

[16] The phrase "have the potential to become public issues" may sound very vague. All issues have the potential to become public ones including the ways that individuals treat each other in family situations. In some societies, familiar, interpersonal issues can easily become inter-clan issues. In some societies, actions between "consenting adults" can become political issues. Sometimes groups or individuals try to make their private concerns become public ones or to insulate their actions from public perusal. Thus raising the question of the possibility of issues becoming public is necessary although we may know issues as such only *ex post facto*.

My understanding of political participation then involves focusing on the different modes of participation used by various groups and individuals as they try to influence each other and Government on public and potentially public issues. It also follows that attempts by individuals and groups to insulate themselves from the influence of others is political participation. Like Verba, I focus on behaviors when concerned with participation. Attitudes are, however, relevant to any discussion of support for a regime. Indeed, a good reason for keeping attitudes and behaviors distinct is to permit us to look at different aspects of regime support. I also include in participation group activity unmediated by Government. Such activity often involves public disputes in developing countries. I emphasize the participant activities of elites as well as those acts of citizens which are designed to insulate themselves from Government or to avoid the consequences of specific policies.

This is a very broad notion of political participation to be sure. The study which follows does not explore all these aspects of participation in equal depth or detail in the Kenya setting. The activities of economic interest groups are not dealt with extensively although I have used recent work done on trade unions, cooperatives, and trade associations. I leave out important non-African groups. In Kenya, even more than in most developing countries, important economic decisions are made by non-citizens some of whom reside outside the country. The large and important non-African sector operates in the political realm too. The analysis below describes African politics in Kenya rather than Kenyan politics as a whole. This leaves out a lot in Kenya for important elites are not receiving consideration. If non-Africans were brought into the analysis, the discussion of class politics that I undertake would be different.[17] Many of the choices that elites give ordinary citizens in Kenya are determined by non-Africans, and non-African elites constrain the choices of African elites too.

I have adopted a different tack than the one of trying to rigorously state a set of definitions in advance and then state hypotheses (which frequently have been suggested by the data which will then confirm them) to confirm or deny. Instead, I hope to clarify some of the issues involved in understanding what political participation in Kenya might usefully mean. This involves trying to find out if attempts to influence Government are critical or if competition directly between groups is what matters most. Also, we shall see that in Kenya it may make very good sense to think about representative Government in a society in which there are great constraints on popular participation as an attempt to affect national governmental patterns from below but at the same time where the populace can choose from among elites, and can organize at subnational levels in a host of important local activities and through local institutions. This focus allows me to inquire about the ways that the availability or non-availability of different kinds of political institutions affects the manner in which individuals and groups contend.

I am aware that when western social scientists began to study developing countries one of the first reactions was against comparative politics as it had been carried on for the study of West European societies; it was a re-

[17] I am grateful to Gary Wasserman for keeping the transnational aspects of Kenyan politics before me. His own study of European farmers emphasizes the importance of non-African actors in Kenya.

action against formal-legal, constitutional studies and that reaction tended to turn against institutional studies as well.[18] Social scientists developed structural-functional analyses and began to look outside formal structures of Government but at the same time the structural-functionalists usually still concentrated on "visible" institutions, e.g., parties, civil services, more recently the military.[19] Analysts of Africa in particular began to voice dissatisfaction with studying institutions. Zolberg went so far as to say that African political life was "an almost institutionless arena with conflict and disorder as its most prominent features."[20] I questioned whether speaking about *the* military makes sense in Africa given the faction-ridden nature of small-scale and frequently unprofessionalized armed forces.[21] However, if one can show a corporate self-interest on the part of an armed forces

[18] For an excellent discussion of trends in the study of comparative politics see Harry Eckstein, "A Perspective on Comparative Politics, Past and Present," in Harry Eckstein and David Apter, eds., *Comparative Politics: A Reader* (New York: The Free Press, 1963), pp. 3-33.

[19] See for example, the work of David Apter, *Ghana in Transition* (New York: Atheneum, 1963), and *The Politics of Modernization* (Chicago: University of Chicago Press, 1965). I have suggested elsewhere why observers in new states continued to focus on parties especially after independence. See Henry Bienen, "One Party Systems in Africa," in Samuel P. Huntington and Clement Moore, eds., *Authoritarian Politics in Modern Societies* (New York: Basic Books, 1970), pp. 99-127.

[20] Aristide Zolberg, "The Structure of Political Conflict in the New States of Tropical Africa," *American Political Science Review*, Vol. 62, No. 1 (1968), p. 70.

[21] See Henry Bienen, ed., *The Military and Modernization* (Chicago: Atherton-Aldine, 1971), pp. 1-33 and Henry Bienen, "The Military and Society in East Africa," paper presented to the Conference on African Armies, Georgetown University, Center for Strategic Studies, May 1970.

organization then it might well make sense to talk about *the* military. Similarly, we should not dismiss the importance of studying institutions because there may be disorder; nor do we have to reify institutions. It has been certainly useful to point out that factions, cliques, patron-client relations are a prominent part of the politics of developing countries. Indeed, we could stand more work on the politics of industrial societies in these terms too. It has also been remedial to point out that cleavage in developing countries cannot be encompassed by ethnicity, class, generation, rural-urban distinctions but must also take into account factional groupings which crosscut these cleavages. There has been a recent explosion of literature which explores factionalism and patron-client relations.[22] It is necessary, however, to explore the pattern of factionalism within institutions when institutions provide the context or partial context for the linking of groups in society.[23]

[22] See for example, John Duncan Powell, "Peasant Society and Clientelist Politics," *American Political Science Review*, Vol. 64, No. 2 (June 1970), pp. 411-425; James C. Scott, "Corruption, Machine Politics and Political Change," *American Political Science Review*, Vol. 63, No. 4 (December 1969), pp. 1142-1158; James C. Scott, "Patron-Client Politics and Political Change," *American Political Science Review*, forthcoming; Rene Lemarchand and Keith Legg, "Political Clientelism and Development: A Preliminary Analysis," *Comparative Politics*, Vol. 4, No. 2 (January 1972), pp. 149-178; Richard Sandbrook, "Patrons, Clients and Factions: New Dimensions of Conflict Analysis in Africa," *Canadian Journal of Political Science*, Vol. 5, No. 1 (March 1972), pp. 104-119; Alex Weingrod, "Patrons, Patronage and Political Parties," *Comparative Studies in Society and History*, Vol. 10 (July 1968), pp. 377-400.

[23] A number of the studies cited above do precisely this. Sandbrook is concerned with trade unions in Kenya; Weingrod with party in Sardinia and Italy; a forthcoming work by Sidney Verba

The first two chapters examine Civil Service and party in Kenya. The aim, however, is not to describe in detail the structure and function of Kenya's Civil Service nor that of KANU.[24] My concern is to explore political control and political participation in Kenya by looking at the way these two institutions operate as vehicles for intra-elite competition, for the channeling of demands upward, for the allocation of resources, and for the imposing of rules and regulations for political behavior. A number of issue areas in Kenyan political life are used to illustrate the setting forth of political demands and the exercise of control. At the same time, these first two chapters begin to analyze the nature of cleavage in Kenya by looking at patterns of authority and factional groupings within the two critical institutions.

The remaining chapters deal more extensively with cleavage in terms of ethnic, class, and factional divisions. They spell out the basis for support of the present regime by looking at the kinds of policies and trade offs that are made. I argue that the Kenyan regime "works" for large numbers of Kenyans despite the gross disparities in power and income between individuals and groups. I also argue that Kenya is a participant society in important respects despite a curtailing of political competition and a fall-off in voting turnout. I also argue that Kenya's leaders are sensitive to rural demands despite the real limits on participation that exist.

and Norman Nie looks at the organizational context of participation and tries to measure the role of organizations and voluntary associations in relation to political participation in the United States.

[24] An excellent description of the Kenya Civil Service can be found in Goran Hyden, Robert Jackson, and John Okumu, eds., *Development Administration: The Kenyan Experience* (Nairobi: Oxford University Press, 1970).

Introduction

Many of the ills that are said to beset African countries appear in Kenya: severe unemployment, rapid urbanization, uneven social and economic development, ethnic conflict, a fragmented ruling party, state protection of vested personal and ethnic interests. For all this, Kenya has maintained a stability of regime. The pattern of rule, that is, the relationships between rulers and ruled, have remained relatively unchanged in the decade since independence. The relationships among ruling institutions have not been much altered and top-level leaders have persisted with a few exceptions. The nature of recruitment into high- and middle-level elite positions has stayed constant. The values underlying the regime, its defense of itself, its claims on its citizens, have also remained consistent. Levels of violence from below and levels of violence by the regime against groups and individuals have been low. In all these respects, it can be said that Kenya has remained stable.

I do not argue that stability is a good thing *per se*, although in Kenya it has been associated with economic development. I do argue that the formation of classes in Kenya, or more accurately, the development of class politics, would be destabilizing. The old colonial regime thought differently. It envisoned that the creation of an African kulak class on the land would provide a stable base for rule and for the maintenance of European economic and political influence in Kenya after independence. I argue that Kenya remains stable because classes have not formed in any clear fashion. By this I do not mean that there are no distinctions of income, status, and privilege in Kenya. These distinctions exist and they tend to be interrelated. Indeed, in Kenya private ownership of property and private trade are more important than

22

in many African countries where control of governmental position or traditional ruling positions are often the major basis for power and wealth. I do mean that politics in Kenya is not determined, political issues are not defined, by economic relationships for all the relevant political strata. Both consciousness of economic ties or shared interests and economically based organizations are weak in urban and rural areas.

In urban areas, the poor and the marginally employed do not constitute an organized political force. Employed workers do not function politically as an organized body. They and the trade union organizations which purport to represent them do not act politically as a class, as organizations and individuals with shared interests. Individual trade unions act to protect economic privileges but they exhibit an economic consciousness of the narrowest sort. It could not even be called trade union consciousness or "economism."

In rural areas, it is hard to know what are the political consequences stemming from distinctions in income and land holding. There appears to be a fairly common life style even for people of somewhat differing income levels who live on the land. Where life-style differences do exist, they are not clearly translated into consistent political attitudes and behaviors. Organizations based on economic distinctions in rural areas do not get institutionalized among either the poor or the better off, though relatively wealthy farmers will capture and use cooperatives or school committees for periods of time. Ethnic ties and patron-client relationships cut across ties based on income differentials or property relations. Of course, wealth is important in forming patron-client groups. Wealth is often more important as the basis for such

23

groups than traditional status in Kenya although sub-
ethnic groups or local cliques are not always dependent
on wealth for their solidarity.

There are rural-urban divisions in Kenya but these
cannot be seen as class divisions in the way that Fanon
sees them.[25] There are no clear-cut rural and urban sectors in Kenya. People move back and forth spatially between rural and urban areas. Politically two distinct
spheres of action do not exist for most people. Nor is
Kenya an example of a parasitical urban sector which
milks a rural population dry.

Kenya is interesting because a buoyant economy, an
industrial sector which is developed, in comparison with
other African countries, and severe population pressure
on the land are not, as yet, associated with a developed
class politics. Political behavior is not determined by
economic relationships for significant groups of the rural
and urban population. Economic elites do try to restrict
access to economic opportunities. But the continued
maintenance of political participation in important local
arenas and in a limited way in the national arena has
worked to keep the political elite responsive to core rural
areas. Responsiveness in turn may have lessened the
impetus to more extensive political participation from
below.

A political process has worked to give the Kenyan
regime support which it has in turn used to embark on
distinctive developmental policies. It is a process rare
enough in developing countries to be worth examining.

[25] Frantz Fanon, *The Wretched of the Earth* (New York:
Grove Press, 1963).

II

Describing Kenya: Administrative and Political Control

I have noted that Kenya has become a controversial country and a symbol of progressive or regressive political and economic evolution and social and economic development, depending on one's point of view and interpretation of the data.[1] Yet there is rather a large amount of agreement on describing Kenya's economy, society, and political institutions. There is less agreement in explaining the features described: why did political institutions evolve in a particular pattern or why did a given economic strategy evolve? There is also less agreement on the relationship of economic and political factors. How, for example, has a fragmented ruling party affected the course of economic development in Kenya and political participation from below? Or, what is the effect of growing economic differentiation among African farmers on participation? What are the consequences of rapid rates of urbanization in Kenya for political organizing in cities and towns?

Thus the meaning of the descriptions of Kenya's

[1] There are positive accounts of Kenya's economic development strategies, but favorable academic evaluations of Kenya's political evolution are less common. The analysis which follows is a minority view in its treatment of participation and support in Kenya. It is certainly true that Kenya has frequently been described in the British and American press as "stable" and "pragmatic" as compared to other African countries.

25

economy, political arrangements, and social structure is hotly debated. To raise questions about the meaning of facts is really to ask how things are interrelated: what are their causes and consequences and contexts. First, I want to describe briefly the Kenya that I think observers agree exist. Then I want to explore interrelationships in order to try to understand that which is described.

Most political studies of Kenya begin by stressing the importance of the colonial legacies for the contemporary period. While African countries in the 1960s were analyzed in terms of party systems, charismatic leaders, ideologies of mobilization or the absence thereof, and, latterly, political machines and patron-client relationships, Kenya was still being discussed largely in terms of its colonial inheritance. Much of the writing on Kenya, even up to the mid-1960s, focused on Mau Mau, its origins and causes, and its consequences for independent Kenya. Closely related to concern with Mau Mau were the treatments of land policy and land reform.[2] One reason for the focus on land and revolt and the colonial past rather than the institutions and ideology of the present as compared to treatments of other African countries was that the colonial experience had marked Kenya as it had few other now independent Black African countries.

Another reason for a certain lack of focus on Kenya's

[2] See, for example, Carl G. Rosberg and John Nottingham, *The Myth of Mau Mau* (New York: Frederick Praeger, 1966); Donald L. Barnett and Karari Njama, *Mau Mau From Within* (London: MacGibbon and Kee, 1966); M.P.K. Sorrenson, *Land Reform in the Kikuyu Country* (London: Oxford University Press, 1967). An exception among major studies was George Bennett and Carl Rosberg, *The Kenyatta Election: Kenya, 1960-61* (London: Oxford University Press, 1961).

contemporary politics was the image that the ruling KANU presented. Because KANU was fragmented and had even less of a central presence and institutional grid than many other African ruling parties, there was a tendency to dismiss party politics, and with it contemporary politics as still being a function of the colonial past.[3] Above all, it was that colonial past which continued to dominate thinking about Kenya because in part it was so traumatic a past and in part because its legacies were, in fact, important and immediate factors in the first decade of independence.

Mau Mau as a violent revolt against colonial rule had been an atypical form of African nationalism in the mid-twentieth century for Africa between the Zambezi and the Sahara. It had pitted African against African as well as African against European. One of its legacies for Kenya was a strong and centralized Civil Service and strong security forces. During Mau Mau, far-reaching changes had taken place in land consolidation and registration among Kikuyu.[4] And Kikuyu participation in politics had been forcibly cut off with the banning until 1959 of political parties in Central Province, the Kikuyu home area.

Mau Mau was an upsurge of Kikuyu activity, but the colonial response had cut Kikuyu off from open political organizing at a crucial time before independence. After

[3] For a discussion of African party systems see Aristide Zolberg, *Creating Political Order: The Party States of West Africa* (Chicago: Rand McNally, 1966), and Henry Bienen, "African One-Party Systems."

[4] See Sorrenson, *op.cit.* The plan to consolidate African land holdings and to establish individual tenure was called the Swynerton Plan. See Colony and Protectorate on Kenya, *African Land Development in Kenya, 1956-62* (Nairobi: Government Printer, 1962).

27

independence, Kikuyu who as a group were relatively well off educationally[5] and who placed high on various indices of modernization[6] found themselves having to reassert political positions by getting control of the major party, KANU, and by Kikuyuizing the armed forces and Civil Service. In other words, the colonial impact was such that Kikuyu were highly mobilized but for a time cut off from political influence. Also, the colonial impact which had been uneven throughout Kenya was most intense among Kikuyu. This meant that Kikuyu had been most affected by education, by the colonial administrative and communication grids, but also that Kikuyu had suffered physically through loss of land and were internally split by the colonial experience. These splits were expressed in a land division that had gone farthest in Kikuyuland so that better-off farmers were frequently Kikuyu but those without land often were Kikuyu also; many urban workers were Kikuyu in Nairobi, on the White Highlands farms of the Rift Valley, and in the towns of Nakuru, Eldoret, and coastal Mombasa, but

[5] Donald Rothchild, "Ethnic Inequalities on Kenya," *Journal of Modern African Studies*, Vol. 7, No. 4 (1969), pp. 689-711, reports that 95 percent of Central Province children were enrolled in primary schools. Central Province is almost entirely Kikuyu in its present boundaries if Nairobi is excluded as it was for this figure. Aside from Nairobi, no other province in Kenya, in 1964 when the figures were taken, had much more than 70 percent enrollment and most were under 50 percent. See *ibid.*, p. 692. Rothchild used data from the *Kenya Education Commission Report, Part II* (Nairobi: Government Printer, 1965), p. 9.

[6] One of the most complete studies of differential resource distribution and the consequences of a colonial impact on resource growth and distribution in a developing country is Edward Soja, *The Geography of Modernization in Kenya* (Syracuse: Syracuse University Press, 1968).

many urban unemployed were also Kikuyu. Economic differentiation had proceeded furthest among Kikuyu than any other African group in Kenya. The benefits and the costs of colonial impact had fallen most heavily on Kikuyu. The Mau Mau experience which some have analyzed in class terms as a struggle of "have" and "have not" Kikuyus also led to a situation where after Mau Mau some Kikuyu were seen as Loyalists and others as rebels.[7] Thus the Mau Mau experience was itself polarizing.

The politics of independent Kenya in good part was to revolve around the share of resources allocated to Kikuyus, and the question of Kikuyu dominance of political life and civil and military service institutions. I shall return to these questions. Here I want to underline that one colonial legacy was the accelerated thrust for Kikuyu participation and domination in the politics of Kenya. Given scarce resources in Kenya, it was likely that economics and ethnicity would interact to inflame tribal tensions in independent Kenyan society. Thus, it also made sense to analyze contemporary Kenya by going back to the colonial period to look at the formation of a Kenyan political elite as well as at the differential distribution of economic and social resources.[8]

One institutional feature of Kenya's political life that can be traced to colonial developments was the emergence of a strong Civil Service. Also directly related to the colonial experience was the emergence of a party

[7] Kaggia's autobiography treats Mau Mau in this fashion. To some extent, Waruihu Itote's *"Mau Mau" General* (Nairobi: East African Publishing House, 1967) does too. Also see Barnett and Njama, *op.cit.*

[8] See Odinga, *op.cit.* and Okumu, *op.cit.* The focus on the colonial past was not peculiar to western social scientists; this framework governed Kenya commentators, social scientists and politicians alike.

29

system characterized by a fission and fusion of contending groups sometimes acting within the framework of two or more parties, sometimes competing inside KANU. The weakly centralized parties with their fluid party alignments must be understood in the context of the relatively strong Civil Service, Kenyatta's personal rule, the nature of ethnic and group conflict in Kenya, and the way that economic and ethnic cleavage overlap.

We ought to be interested in the effects of an institutional structure both on the processes through which resources are distributed and on the direction of the distributions. We also want to know how an institutional structure affects the way that people participate in politics and how the emergence of new groups in politics or the closing off from politics of old ones affects institutional structures. The analysis of Civil Service and party in Kenya provides us with a way of looking at participation and distribution of resources. Also, the analysis of Civil Service and party is a way of cutting into questions about ethnicity and class.

A. The Strength of the Civil Service

At the time of independence in 1963, Kenya had a relatively well-developed Civil Service. The size of the Kenya Civil Service was about one-third larger than the then Tanganyika's, although the latter had about 10 percent larger population. Kenya's Civil Service was more developed than elsewhere in former British colonial territories in East Africa because it had been constructed to provide services for a white-settler population[9] and because during the Mau Mau period both provincial ad-

[9] District councils depended for revenues on taxes collected by the provincial administration.

ministration and security forces in particular had been strengthened to deal with law and order problems.[10] Moreover, during Mau Mau large numbers of Kikuyu had been forcibly repatriated from the Rift Valley— where they had worked on white-owned farms and from Nairobi where they constituted a sizable proportion of the labor force—to the Kikuyu home areas or reserves in Central Province. The collection of many thousands of people and their forced migration back to home areas necessitated the development of a Civil Service structure to cope with the problems entailed.[11] When the colonial Government used Kikuyu opponents of the regime to push across land registration and consolidation in Kikuyu areas and to forcibly villagize the population, again, security forces and general administration had to be elaborated.[12]

[10] From 1952 to 1957, 419,000 arrests were made in Kenya. The population was under 9 million at the time. A. W. Southall, "The Growth of Urban Society," in Stanley Diamond and Fred Burke, eds., *The Transformation of East Africa* (New York: Basic Books, 1964), pp. 463-493.

[11] The percentage of Kikuyu and Embu and Meru (related tribes) in the total labor force fell from 47 percent to 22 percent between 1963 and 1956. The number of Luo, Luyha, and Kisii rose from 27 percent to 38 percent and Kamba rose from 18 percent to 28 percent in Nairobi. A swing back came about after the Emergency so that by the 1962 Census, the number of Kikuyu, Embu, and Meru males in Nairobi was 44 percent while Luo, Luyha, and Kisii males in Nairobi were 33 percent and Kamba males were 17 percent. (Males would not be perfectly correlated with total labor force figures in Nairobi.) *Ibid.*, p. 493.

[12] As Thomas Mulusa, "Central Government and Local Authorities," in Hyden, Okumu, and Jackson, pp. 233-251, points out, the provincial administration was particularly elaborate in Central Province. This was the Kikuyu homeland where Nairobi is situated. "Nairobi, granted the status of a city in 1950, was virtually reduced to a set of villages . . . effectively administered

31

There was also an interest in getting greater agricultural production out of both the settler areas and the African ones during World War II and afterward. In Tanganyika this concern had led to the ill-fated Ground Nut scheme; in Kenya both expansion of the European sector and transformation of the African subsistence sector were pushed. Thus not only was there a general expansion of the Civil Service between 1945 and 1955 from 14,000 to 45,000 (in rounded figures) but also in technical ministries the Civil Service expanded rapidly. There were 298 in the staff of the Agricultural Department at all levels in 1945 and 2,519 in 1958. The African Land Development Department did not exist in 1945; it had 477 people in 1958.[13] By the end of 1965, the Civil Service had grown to 63,000 and 92 percent were Kenyan citizens; overwhelmingly they were Africans. By 1969, the Civil Service had increased to 77,000 with almost 95 percent citizens.

The growth in size of the Civil Service after independence was in part a response to economic needs. That is,

---

by the central government through district officers in various suburban areas" (p. 239). Local authorities in most areas lost most of their powers to provincial administration during the Emergency in Kenya from 1952 to 1955. In Kiambu District, a Kikuyu heartland area, there were one district commissioner and two district officers in 1952. In 1956, there were one district commissioner, twenty-six district officers, and eleven district assistants.

[13] These figures for the technical departments are from Cherry Gertzel, *The Politics of Independent Kenya* (Nairobi: East African Publishing House, 1970), p. 22. The discussion of the Kenya Civil Service relies heavily on Gertzel, especially pp. 20-39 and 166-173. I have also used Hyden, Jackson, and Okumu, *op.cit.*, esp. Goran Hyden, "Basic Civil Service Characteristics," pp. 3-32; Henry Bienen, "Economic Environment," pp. 43-62; and John Okumu, "Socio-Politico Setting," pp. 25-42.

the economy of Kenya was perceived to have potential for growth and was in fact growing. Total GNP expanded at 6.8 percent cumulatively at constant prices for the 1964-68 period. Expansion and economic change also created personnel needs. As the Kenya Government implemented policies designed to Africanize trade and business, personnel were required to administer licensing and loan programs. As Government proliferated marketing boards and regulatory agencies, the size of the Civil Service had to expand. Government agricultural improvement policies led to increases in field staff.[14]

However, as Hyden pointed out, the growth of the Kenya Civil Service can be viewed only partially as a response of Government to economic growth and growth potential and to the concern for structural transformation of the economy. "It [growth] must also be viewed as the consequences of the autonomous goal-setting character of the civil service itself. . . ."[15] Civil servants were trying to expand their empires. But as the public sector employment grew from over 188,000 in 1965 to almost 222,000 in 1968, at a time when employment in the private sector was declining from 402,000 to 387,000, the expansion of the Civil Service must also be understood in political terms.[16] The public sector ac-

[14] Jon Moris has described in detail the available structure of agricultural extension services and personnel in "The Agrarian Revolution in Central Kenya: A Study of Farm Innovation in Embu District," Northwestern University, Dissertation submitted to the Department of Anthropology, 1970, University Microfilms, Ann Arbor.

[15] Hyden, *op.cit.*, p. 9.

[16] Bienen, "Economic Environment," p. 49. See *Economic Survey, 1969* (Nairobi: Government Printer, 1969), Table 8.2, p. 120. Public sector employment figures include employees of central government, parastatal organizations, East African Com-

counted in 1969 for over 36 percent of all employed and was a critical sector for absorbing the rising would-be employed, and in particular the well-educated would-be employed. Civil Service was second only to teaching as the career preference of Kenyan university students.[17] Not only were there severe pressures from the better educated and from civil servants trying to increase the size of their departments for bureaucratic power and leverage, but the ethnic pressures were strong to expand positions to let individuals in for a slice of the pie through pressuring Civil Service for jobs and services. Another consideration working for growth was the age structure in the Civil Service. Because the Civil Service was Africanized belatedly and then expanded rapidly in the 1950s and early 1960s it was heavy with relatively young people throughout its ranks. This meant that normal attrition patterns were not working. The only way to bring new and often better-qualified technical personnel and better-educated general administrators into the system was to expand it.

Within this expanding Civil Service, the provincial administration played a critical role during Mau Mau, the security forces expanded rapidly as did the provincial administration, but even the police was subordinate to the provincial administration in matters concerning law and order during the emergency.[18] At independence, Kenya had a provincial administration staffed not by young graduates just out of university but by experienced junior peo-

---

munity Services organizations, and local government. The important political actors are civil servants in the central government.

[17] Joel D. Barkan, "What Makes East African Students Run," *Transition* (Kampala), Vol. 7, No. 37 (1968), p. 28, Table 5.

[18] Gertzel, *Politics of Independent Kenya*, p. 23.

ple who had served on African district councils or in the colonial provincial administration. Many such people saw themselves as taking power within the structure of the administration. The provincial commissioners had operated as heads of Government in Kenya's provinces; they were the agents of executive control for the Governor as they were to become subsequently for the President of Kenya. Even during the short interlude 1963-64 when Kenya operated under a system of regionalism in the Majimbo Constitution when the provincial commissioners were heads of Civil Service in the regions and responsible to elected regional authorities or assemblies, Kenya remained a centralized administrative system. *De facto* the central ministries kept the critical functions of Government, and the provincial administration often bypassed the regional assemblies.[19] There was never a full implementation of the Majimbo Constitution and control functions as well as development initiatives continued to be vested in the provincial administration. Indeed, the provincial administration was itself much more of a coordinator and initiator in both realms than the technical ministries as compared to other African countries.

Thus even when Kenya was in theory decentralized through regional assemblies, the political realities were different. Prime Minister Kenyatta ruled through his provincial administration. In December 1964, Kenya became both a Republic and a *de facto* one-party state when the opposition Kenya African Democratic Union (KADU) crossed the floor and its members joined KANU. The powers of the regions were abolished and the ex-

[19] The most complete discussion of the provincial administration is Cherry Gertzel, "The Provincial Administration in Kenya," *Journal of Commonwealth Political Studies,* Vol. 4, No. 3 (November 1966), pp. 201-215.　1807596

ecutive head of Government became a President in place of a Prime Minister.[20] In the course of 1964-66, the constitutional structure of Kenya was altered to produce a yet more centralized system. The President's emergency powers were enlarged; the Executive's power continued to encroach on those of Legislature, and the provincial administration worked directly to the Office of the President and became his primary agent for exerting political control throughout Kenya.

As Gertzel points out, the provincial administration, led by district and provincial commissioners, assumed again most of the responsibilities in theory but in practice only partially lost to local or county councils and regional assemblies in 1963.[21] Indeed, for many civil servants in the provincial administration, the Majimbo period of Kenya regionalism reinforced feelings of superiority to politicians. The politicians they were most in contact with were regional and local ones. The central ministries also resumed full control of their activities in the regions and districts with the exception of certain educational, health, and road services. Even these functions were taken away from the county councils with the Local Government Transfer of Functions Bill of October 1969, when primary education, health, and secondary road

[20] Gertzel, *Politics of Independent Kenya*, p. 34. The President as Head of Government remained Head of Cabinet; he had to be an elected member of the Legislature. The Legislature became unicameral instead of bicameral in December 1966, when the Senate and the House of Representatives were merged. For a constitutional history of Kenya see D. Ghai and J.P.W.B. McAuslan, *Public Law and Political Change in Kenya* (London: Oxford University Press, 1972). For the administrative and executive aspects, see especially pp. 177-309.

[21] Gertzel, *Politics of Independent Kenya*, p. 36. For a discussion of local authorities see Mulusa, "Central Government."

maintenance were transferred to central government ministries which already indirectly controlled these functions.[22] (The Ministry of Local Government had direct control over local authorities by 1965.) The continued weakness of local Government as manifested in county councils and the fragmentary and intermittent presence of KANU in many districts accentuated district and provincial commissioners' tendencies to think of themselves as leaders of districts and provinces.

All commentators agree that Kenya's provincial administration is centralized in the President's Office and carries out a wide array of functions compared to other African civil services. Not only were the provincial administrative officers collecting taxes on behalf of local authorities, they also chaired land boards, loan boards, agricultural committees, licensing committees, self-help committees. They were given major responsibilities for development in a province and district and when the Ministry of Economic Planning and Development set up structures for planning and plan implementation, the provincial administration became the agent of development as coordinator of other Civil Service personnel. Weaknesses in field representation of the Ministry of Economic Planning and Development meant that the provincial and district commissioners filled certain technical roles. But most important for the centralization of authority and the wide range of functions carried out by provincial administration was the political power of the commissioners themselves and the reliance of the President on them. In other words, while there was a colonial legacy which had been manifested in the structural dominance of the provincial administration, it was a set of choices

[22] Mulusa, p. 251.

at the center which gave the provincial administration ongoing political power. The Office of the President defined the nature of the power of its provincial administration. The provincial administration was the major agent and spokesman of the Government and it also had to be involved in local politics. But it did not "make" policy at the center although powerful provincial commissioners did argue for their own priorities.

The commissioners have understood themselves to be powerful men, powerful vis-à-vis party people in their areas and vis-à-vis the representatives of the central ministries and elected officials like MPs, district councilors, and even ministers when the latter were operating in a commissioner's province or district and involving themselves in provincial affairs. But they do not see themselves as powerful central actors, setting priorities for the nation. They are prefects but they are not national figures in their own right; they do not build up independent bases of political power outside of the regions to which they are posted. The district commissioners in particular are moved around. While it is true that some members of the provincial administration resigned from the Civil Service to stand for Parliament in 1969, the provincial and district commissioners are not overtly political officials like Tanzania's regional and area commissioners.[23] They do not shy away from involving themselves in political problems but they do not define themselves as political people. While they see their power as being delegated from the Office of the President and President Kenyatta personally, and while they rely on the his-

[23] For a discussion of Tanzania's regional and area commissioners see Henry Bienen, *Tanzania: Party Transformation and Economic Development* (Princeton: Princeton University Press, 1970), pp. 307-333.

38

torical tradition of a strong provincial administration in Kenya, they circumscribe their own roles. A lot of politics that does go on goes on outside their purview by their own choice; indeed, the provincial and district commissioners were often reluctant to get involved in intra-KANU squabbles and had to be ordered to do so by the President. And when district commissioners were involved in disqualifying Kenya People's Union (KPU) candidates for local office in 1968 they were frequently unhappy about the role they had been given.[24] Some were unhappy about being called to a KANU meeting held in Nakuru in 1968 to discuss the way the Civil Service would relate to party politics. President Kenyatta has used the provincial administration as the major agent of Government because it was for him the most reliable institution and one which he could control personally in a way that we shall see was impossible to do with KANU.

No one doubts that the Civil Service, and the provincial administration in particular, has been a strong institution in Kenyan life and that it is the main instrument of social control. The Civil Service is also the major vehicle for political participation from below for three reasons: (1) it is the major point of contact with Government for most Kenyans; (2) it is given social and economic transformation tasks; (3) it is explicitly told by top political authorities that it should be a channel for local demands and that it should try to handle local grievances because the political leadership has determined to bypass an unreliable and fragmented ruling party. A visitor to provincial, district, or divisional headquarters can find people waiting to see representatives of the central ministries and the provincial administration

[24] From interviews with commissioners in 1968-69.

in order to state their problems and to involve them in their grievances. KANU officials come to headquarters to petition also. The scenes of people waiting to see a district commissioner are similar to the lines in district *bomas* or headquarters in Tanzania where people wait on area commissioners. In Tanzania, however, people are waiting to see a party official as well as a representative of Government in the person of the commissioner. And they also queue at TANU offices to see party chairmen about the granting of favors and the settlement of disputes.

Well-placed people in Kenya, those of wealth and power, will involve themselves in high-level KANU politics, and middle-level elites will engage in internal KANU struggles in order to be better placed to pursue their advantage. High-level elites will also try to deal directly with the President or more frequently will deal with officials in his Office. But for most Kenyans, the Civil Service is the main point of contact with public authority. Civil servants in the technical ministries, especially agriculture, provide information about Government's policies and they provide assistance and resources to farmers. Representatives of some of the agricultural and marketing boards do this too.

Chiefs, who are the grass-roots agents of the provincial administration,[25] call meetings or *barazas*—which are probably the main point of contact between the rural population and the regime, even taking KANU meetings into account. The latter require permission from district

[25] The hierarchy of the provincial administration is, descending: provincial commissioner; district commissioner; district officer; senior district assistant; district assistant; chief; subchief. Village headmen are not salaried employees of the provincial administration.

commissioners which is not always granted.[26] But chiefs can get their meetings held. The chief explains Government policies at these barazas. And they are held frequently. In Vihiga, a division in western Kenya which is very densely settled and which has a population of close to 300,000, one observer states that there are 280 barazas each week.[27] In a year, chiefs held 288 barazas and subchiefs held over 3,000 in Vihiga.[28] The main attendants at such meetings were elders and village headmen and farmers. Nyangira reports that most frequently subsistence farmers were the majority of those in attendance. But they were elderly, often illiterate, and marginal for the development programs being espoused. At the barazas appeals are made for loyalty to the nation and the President. Government's plans are noted. Pleas are made for the payment of taxes and contributions to self-help schemes. The barazas frequently are tax-collecting devices. Police check tax receipts during them and not-so-voluntary contributions to self-help schemes are gathered. Nyangira states that the baraza still has an aura of the colonially enforced meeting. A policeman stands by the chief with his baton. The symbol of order and control, the chief, becomes the explainer of Government actions. The chief's baraza is the instrument of mobilization and control at the grass roots. But since the provincial administration has expended tremendous amounts of time and energy on graduated personal tax collection,

[26] Such permission is required for MPs who want to address meetings also.

[27] Kenya is divided for administrative purposes into provinces, districts, divisions, subdivisions and locations.

[28] I am relying on Nicholas Nyangira's "Chiefs' Barazas as Agents of Administration and Political Change," IDS, Staff Paper No. 80, Nairobi, July 1970.

some have wondered whether its developmental role has been compromised.

In fact, the provincial administration is carrying out roles which are not easily compatible when it acts as the implementer of centrally established policies and extractor of resources on the one hand and agent for social transformation and political participation on the other. The Civil Service as a whole is exhorted to be innovative, to get people to change old habits and to make it clear that incentives for change are available and also to listen to grievances and advance them upward in the chain of command. Representatives of some ministries are designated as representatives of constituents. This is clear for community development officers. But regional and district officials in the Ministries of Trade and Agriculture will see themselves in this light too. Trade officials who have the mission to increase African participation in trade will try to accommodate local demands and will get involved in local politics. The allocation of trade licenses and loans is, of course, a politically charged affair. But the representatives of the Ministry of Trade in the regions and districts do not always understand the constellation of politics at their level and they do not have the political power and resources to handle their problems. The district and provincial commissioners invariably get drawn into licensing and loan disputes.

There has also been an attack on the Civil Service in its "development administration" guise. The provincial administration in particular is said to have incompatible functions of social control and social transformation. Critics of Kenya's administration have argued that it is recruited and organized for maintenance of order and control, not for innovation or stimulation of participation from below. The highly centralized and bureaucratic nature of the Civil Service, it is said, militates against its being a change-oriented institution.[29]

Government conducted its own Commission of Inquiry into the Civil Service to review both its structure and remuneration levels and more broadly to examine "whether the Civil Service inherited at Independence, modified in some respects and staffed with Kenyans, committed to the ideals of nation-building, is in fact well adapted to the task of development as it actually presents itself in the 1970's?"[30] This Commission frankly recognized that KANU does not formulate new policies and that other institutions which could contribute to policy formulation were relatively few and weak. Thus the Civil Service was called on to identify and solve national problems. But the Commission recognized that though there has been a clear shift in the focus of interest toward development the average civil servant followed old procedures. The problem has been exacerbated because the strong system of field administration expressed in the provincial administration was never designed around the concept of planned development and project management.[31]

The Civil Service has been criticized for being unable to handle political demands in a disinterested way. It is said to be a major interest group in the political process. It is also asserted that the Civil Service is without the local roots which only a political party can have and

[29] For the public administration arguments pro and con see Hyden, Jackson, and Okumu, *op.cit.*, and John Nellis, "Is the Kenyan Bureaucracy Developmental?" *African Studies Review*, Vol. 14, No. 3 (December 1971), pp. 389-402.

[30] *Report of the Commission of Inquiry* (Public Service Structure and Remuneration Commission, 1971) also known as the Ndegwa Commission (Nairobi: Government Printer, 1971), pp. 2-3.

[31] *Ibid.*, pp. 21-22.

which allows a party to understand and channel and respond to local demands.

We can examine two issue areas, the role of local government councils and the question of self-help or Harambee schools, in order to see how the Civil Service tries to respond to and control local demands. We can also examine the idea that the Civil Service is a corporate group which acts in its own interest.

B. CONTROLLING LOCAL COUNCILS

These arguments are heard even more in the land since 1970 when the central government took over the three basic services which county councils, the major elected body in the rural areas, had responsibility for. Primary education, which had taken up 62.5 percent on the total county council expenditure of 16 million pounds in 1969 and which had essentially bankrupted the councils, and roads and health were all taken over by central Government.[32] Together they had accounted for over 80 percent of total county council expenditure. In 1968, local councils were spending 26 percent of total governmental expenditure. Many, but not all county councils, had become financially in disarray and Government took over their main functions on the grounds that they could not provide services

[32] For a discussion of local government in Kenya see Mulusa, "Central Government"; V. P. Diejomaoh, "Financing Local Government Authorities in Kenya," IDS Discussion Paper No. 96, Nairobi, September 1970; Goran Hyden, "Local Government Reform in Kenya," *East Africa Journal*, Vol. 7, No. 4 (April 1970), pp. 19-24; W.J.W. Bowring, "Competitive Politics in East African Local Government," *The Journal of Developing Areas*, Vol. 5 (October 1970), pp. 43-60.

and had failed to solve financial problems.[33] While this is true, Government had also taken away from the councils their major revenue-getting devices. And it had become clear that central leaders preferred to end local autonomy over crucial areas.

Not all the reasons of central leaders had to do with good administrative procedures. In 1968, Government refused to allow fair municipal elections to take place.[34] The then existing opposition party, KPU, had its candidates barred through administrative procedures. It was claimed that they had made out their papers incorrectly when filing. It was the regional administration which acted as the agent for squashing the possibilities of free elections and a number of district commissioners were unhappy about the political use made of them.[35] While some have claimed that the KANU Government feared a good KPU showing, there is little evidence that outside of Luo areas the KPU would have done well in municipal elections. I would argue instead that the KANU Govern-

[33] Richard Stren, "Local Government in Kenya: The Limits of Development Planning," paper prepared for delivery at the Annual Meeting of the African Studies Association, Montreal, October 15-18, 1969, p. 3. Some councils had been unable to pay teachers. Accounting procedures were not always strict and corruption did exist in some councils.

[34] Kenya has had a tiered system of local government. There are seven municipal councils: Nairobi, Mombasa, Nakuru, Kisumu, Thika, Eldoret, and Kitale. There are thirty-three county councils. These county councils sometimes coincide with, sometimes overlap, district councils. There are eighteen urban councils and fifty-four area councils. The latter two categories fall under county council jurisdiction. The municipal councils do not.

[35] Personal interviews with provincial and district commissioners in 1968-69.

ment was more generally interested in tightening controls over political activity. Local councils had often given prominent politicians a local political base. They provided an important arena for factional politics.[36] Alliances were made between the center and the rural areas; politicians poached on each other's territory. The county councils were distributors of patronage through their hiring and development activities. Intense fighting within KANU went on between those who controlled county or municipal councils and often different groups who controlled a KANU district branch or important trade union. Government found competition at the local level messy at best and dangerous for local stability and even at times threatening to national stability as local factionalism ramified up to the national level. Government refused to let independents stand for either local election or Parliament out of concern for internal factionalism within KANU more than out of fear of opposition parties. At first, an attempt was made to use KANU to discipline local factions. When this failed, legislation was imposed in 1968.[37]

The treatment of local councils then was part of a general response aimed at setting limits to participation from below. It grew out of the same concerns which led to attempts to control the trade union movement after independence. Then Government's supervision and reg-

[36] For an excellent account of factional politics on the Coast see Richard Stren, "Factional Politics and Central Control in Mombasa, 1960-1969," *Canadian Journal of African Studies* (Winter 1970), pp. 33-56.

[37] The minutes of an important KANU meeting in Mombasa state that the district chairmen of the party and MPs should supervise the selection of local government candidates. Often, chairmen and MPs could not agree among themselves.

ulation of the trade unions were essentially a response to political activities pursued by union leaders from independent bases of power. However, Government's regulation was justified by the need to control wages and strike levels that would benefit the economy as a whole.[38] Interestingly, one of the main architects of both Government's administrative juggling with the 1968 municipal elections and the legislative and administrative regulation of the trade union movement was Tom Mboya.[39] Since neither Mboya nor Kenyatta himself was able to impose party discipline on the trade unions or on local councils or on local KANU bodies, the Civil Service was used to carry out legislation and to deal administratively with the problems. The Civil Service was given the mission to try to channel demands, for the county councils

[38] Richard Sandbrook has written valuable studies of the Kenya trade union movement. See his "State and the Development of the Trade Unions," in Hyden, Jackson, and Okumu, *op.cit.*, pp. 252-295, and his "Patrons, Clients, and Unions: The Labour Movement and Political Conflict in Kenya," *Journal of Commonwealth Political Studies*, Vol. 9 (March 1972), pp. 13-27.

[39] Mboya held a number of important Cabinet posts and he was Secretary General of KANU until his assassination in 1969. He was Minister of Labour in the first government formed as a KANU-KADU coalition in 1962. He had risen to power through the labor movement. He introduced the Trade Unions (Amendment) Act in 1964 when he was Minister for Justice and Constitutional Affairs. The bill made the ousting of incumbent leaders and the formation of splinter unions more difficult. Sandbrook, "State and the Development of Trade Unions," p. 279. Mboya suggested that it was preferable to deal administratively with the 1968 municipal elections rather than ban the KPU or not permit the election to take place. Thus opposition and party factionalism were controlled through Civil Service manipulation of candidate nominations.

47

had responded to felt needs. They had gone bankrupt trying to take on tasks which people wanted carried out. The overwhelming demand in the rural areas has been for expansion of schooling opportunities. Farmers have sold off their grade cattle and mortgaged land in order to get school fees.[40] People are willing to make great sacrifices to send their children to school because they think education is essential for a chance to increase one's income. Even though people are becoming increasingly aware of the secondary and primary school-leaver problem and know that graduates of lower schools will not necessarily get good jobs, the possibility that they may get such a job is still compelling.[41]

Kenya has a severe unemployment problem and a low-level trained manpower glut. The Civil Service now has to come to grips with the education-employment-rural-urban migration imbalances. Thus the school issue provides a good illustration of the problem for the Civil Service in trying to channel demands at the local level.

[40] Moris, "Agrarian Revolution," p. 212. Even in a sample of employed and unemployed in Nairobi and Mombasa and in peri-urban areas nearby, education was mentioned as a most important problem by 40 percent. This was second only to unemployment, mentioned by 33 percent. From Raymond Hopkins, unpublished "Code Book for the Kenyan Study of Social Mobilization and Political Participation," (1971), p. ii. I am grateful to Professor Hopkins for the use of this study.

[41] The phenomenon is parallel to the one Harris and Todaro have drawn our attention to in rural-urban migration patterns. The migrant to the city plays a lottery. He knows the chances of getting a job in the city may be against him, but the alternative of staying on the land is bleak and taking a chance on a job is worth it because the return is so great if a job is obtained. See John Harris and Michael P. Todaro, "Urban Unemployment in East Africa: An Economic Analysis of Policy Alternatives," *East African Economic Review*, Vol. 4 (1968), pp. 17-36.

C. HARAMBEE SCHOOLS: LOCAL DEMANDS AND GOVERNMENT RESPONSE

Kenya has had a remarkable expansion of primary and secondary school places since independence. Government first stimulated and then tried to control a phenomenon remarkable in its own right: the Harambee or self-help secondary school development.

President Kenyatta once said that it took the British seventy years to build 141 secondary schools in Kenya. "In the three years in which we came to power, the number has increased by 141."[42] Indeed, the Kenyatta Government can point to a great expansion in both primary and secondary school enrollment. In 1960, there were 725,865 students in the first through eighth primary years and there were 17,157 who had made it to that eighth year. In 1965, the numbers were over 1 million and over 150,000 respectively.[43] Kenya shifted to a seven-year primary school program and by 1970 had 1.3 million in primary school and 160,000 in the last year of primary school. The number of students in secondary school forms I-IV was also increasing: from 5,409 in 1965 to 31,796 in 1968 and 60,700 in 1970.[44]

The expansion of the school system was by no means an unmixed blessing. During the period of school ex-

[42] Cited by Kenneth Prewitt, "Schooling, Stratification and Equality: Notes for Research," IDS Paper, Nairobi, n.d., p. 15.

[43] Figures are from Sheldon Weeks, *Divergence in Educational Development* (New York: Teachers College Press, 1967), p. 25, Table I. In 1965, approximately 150,000 students took the Kenya Primary Examination: 117,663 were from Primary VII and 32,485 were remaining from Primary VIII.

[44] *Ibid.* The number who received certificate passes at the end of Form IV went from 649 to 4,557 and then to 9,100 in 1970.

pansion, two critical things were happening in the wage sector. Although the economy expanded, wage employment off the land declined in absolute numbers. And, while the number of students who were sitting the Kenya Primary Examination (KPE) for entrance into secondary school went up tenfold, jobs which KPE matriculates could get in 1964 now required some secondary schooling.[45] Even though primary and secondary schooling was not free in Kenya, the employment problem did not lessen the pressures for schooling. It pushed them upward if anything into a greater demand for secondary schooling. Many of the primary school students were at the same time not getting a satisfactory education. The rapid expansion of the primary schools led to a situation where in 1965, 35 percent of primary school teachers were themselves untrained; three-quarters of these 35 percent had not gone into secondary school.

The expansion of primary schooling led to another difficult problem. The number of secondary school places was insufficient to absorb would-be entrants. Moreover,

[45] The problem of school expansion in East Africa has been dealt with by a number of people. Weeks, *op.cit.*; L. Gray Cowan, *The Costs of Learning: The Politics of Primary Education in Kenya* (New York: Teachers College Press, 1970); John Anderson, "Education for Self Reliance," IDS Discussion Paper No. 67, Nairobi, September 1968; James Sheffield, ed., *Education, Employment and Rural Development* (Nairobi: East African Publishing House, 1967). Tanzania, more than Kenya, has tried to cope with the education problem by stressing curricular changes and the need to develop an education system suitable for those who will remain on the land. Neither teachers nor parents seem to like this any better in Tanzania than they would in Kenya. There has developed recently in Kenya a village polytechnic movement which might develop into an alternative to Kenya's present formal education system in rural areas.

the number of places available in secondary schools was uneven across the country. The Kikuyu areas where the pressure was greatest had places for only 7.1 percent of those who might have possibly graduated from primary school. Nairobi had more places (for 37 percent) and so did the backward areas because, while the latter did not have many schools, they also did not have the pressures that Nairobi and Central Province (Kikuyuland) had.[46] Government planned that about 10 percent of those who sat the KPE would go on to secondary schools which were aided by the Government. Parents and students had other ideas. Many students repeated the primary examination, hoping for better scores a second or third time around. Some have gone back to Standard VII or even Standard VI. Some private schools have sprung up. But the main development has been the growth of the Harambee school system.

"Harambee" has been translated as "Let's pull together."[47] President Kenyatta begins, ends, and liberally punctuates his speeches with "Harambee," and it has become a slogan for Kenyans. Kenyans pull together to build unaided secondary schools in rural areas and then they try to get Government to accredit them, send teach-

[46] The undeveloped Northeastern Province had places for 35 percent of the primary school-leavers; Coast Province, 18.6 percent; Eastern, 6.7 percent; Nyanza (the Luo area), 6.6 percent; Western, 9.1 percent; and Rift Valley, 8.9 percent. These figures are from James Sheffield, *Education in the Republic of Kenya* (Washington: Government Printing Office, 1971), p. 24.

[47] In 1963, Kenyatta made a speech in which he referred to Karambee, a Kikuyu term for pulling together. This has come to be known as Harambee in Kenya. See W. B. Mukuria, "Harambee Secondary Schools—An Aspect of Self-Help Projects in Kikuyu Division, Kenya," The University of East Africa, University Examinations, Dar es Salaam, 1969.

ers, help with salaries, or best of all, take over the Harambee school entirely. The Harambee schools have been largely a Kikuyu phenomena, but not exclusively so. In very densely settled areas outside Kikuyuland where land is scarce and there is a high premium put on education so that children will be able to leave the district, Harambee schools have been built, e.g., in Kakamega district among the Luyha. The idea is that children will get schooling, become wage earners, and return with fresh capital. They usually do send money back if they obtain jobs.

Anderson and Mukuria have traced the origins of self-help activities in Kenya back to age-grade structures and patterns of communal government and responsibility which were featured in many of Kenya's traditional societies.[48] Some Kikuyu had rebelled against the colonial educational system and had established their own schools through the Independent African School movement in the 1930s and 1940s. In the 1960s, Kenyan leaders went to the rural areas and told the people that self-help activities should be taken up. People responded by building secondary schools.

The Harambee schools grew rapidly, although not all unaided schools are Harambee schools. Thus by 1967, there were 361 unaided schools, up from 32 in 1963 and 201 in 1966. Of these, 247 were considered Harambee. The other 114 were commercial, private, tutorial, or special religious schools. In 1968, growth slowed and there were 369 unaided schools. During this period,

[48] Anderson, *op.cit.* and Mukuria, *op.cit.* The latter notes that Kikuyu traditionally did cooperative work in cultivating, thatching, etc., known as *Ngwatio* which has a connotation of communalism and mutuality.

Government-maintained secondary schools went to 232 in 1968.[49]

The Harambee schools have been an expensive proposition for rural people. It has been estimated that 53 percent of self-help contributions went for educational projects. The valuation of self-help is notoriously tricky. It is estimated that in Central Province more than $2 million was collected for self-help in a year. The total county council collection from Graduated Personal Tax was about $1.5 million in the same year. The Harambee schools have also been expensive as compared to Government schools. They charge as much as $120 in fees as compared with $65 in Government-approved boarding schools and $28 in Government-maintained and assisted day schools. School fees and donations to schools appear to be the largest charge against most family budgets in progressive Kikuyu areas. I have already mentioned that cattle may be sold off to pay costs; plowing and spraying may be delayed too. The educational services performed by the Harambee schools, however, have been variable. The output of the Harambee schools depends on how well planned they are, whether money continues to flow in for salaries after school construction has occurred, and how well administered the school is.

The administration of Harambee schools is by committee. Usually, a small group of influential people will call a meeting. Chiefs, headmasters, religious leaders will attend. They and prominent traders or local civil servants or better-off farmers will form the committee.[50] Committees may waive school fees but sometimes they refuse to

[49] Sheffield, *Education*, p. 27.
[50] Anderson, *op.cit.*, p. 15.

do so for the poor. Yet everyone may pay contributions to the Harambee school. If fees are not waived for the poor, the inequalities are exacerbated. Thus the question of who will attend Harambee schools and who will pay fees becomes a highly charged one. The importance of the Harambee schools is underscored. Consider that of the 147,000 primary school-leavers in 1967, only 15,000 had found places in Government-aided secondary schools and 12,000 had found places in Harambee schools, while 6,000 found places in other unaided schools, 15,000 repeated primary school, 4,000 were in some further training and only 20,000 were estimated to have found permanent employment, while 75,000 did not find employment.[51]

The Harambee schools have become a major political concern in the rural areas also because they become the focus for political rivalries between leaders of local communities and because local leaders try to intervene with political leaders and the Ministry of Education at the center in order to strengthen themselves in their localities. There will be a struggle over where the school is sited. And once a decision is made to proceed with a school, the control of its committee may be contentious. Some schools have come to grief because of infighting over the school committee. Different factions will support or oppose schools depending on what positions their opponents take. Or even more common, if one prominent leader is supporting a Harambee school, others will feel compelled to do

[51] *Ibid.*, p. 3. We can see their importance by looking at figures from one important division—the Kikuyu division in Central Province. In 1967, 2,287 students sat for the Kenya Primary Examination. Eighty got into Government-aided secondary schools. Two hundred and seventy more entered Harambee schools. Two hundred repeated. Mukuria, *op.cit.*

the same for a new school. In one case, Bildad Kaggia, a prominent leader in Muran'ga District opposed the building of Harambee schools on the grounds that schools were the responsibility of Government and that it was not clear how the secondary school-leavers would be absorbed, given Government's failure to deal with unemployment. His major opponent in the district, J. K. Kiano, a Cabinet member and at the time Minister of Education, claimed that Kaggia opposed self-help and Harambee schools simply to be obstructionist. Kiano claimed that small-holder interests were the same as those of the wealthy—a claim frequently made by regime spokesmen, and that Harambee schools were a concrete expression of the commonality of interest. Indeed, elite support for the Harambee schools was often put in terms of the need for unity. And the schools did help bring a level of participation on the part of small farmers that elites found useful.[52]

Sometimes KANU has organizational reality only when it becomes involved in local self-help projects. In some divisions, KANU will be highly organized around Harambee school projects, water projects, dispensaries, and clinics. The grass-roots strength may be great. Elsewhere, KANU may have no reality at the grass roots and not be involved at all in local projects.[53]

The Civil Service is given a difficult task in this con-

[52] For a discussion of factionalism in Muran'ga District and the role of Kaggia, there is an unpublished study by Geoffrey Lamb, "Politics and Administration in Muran'ga District Kenya," University of Sussex, 1968. I have benefited from this study.

[53] Mukuria, *op.cit.*, examined two localities and found that KANU was highly organized in one whereas in the other community 75 percent of the people questioned wondered whether KANU existed there at all. Party officials were not known locally to members of Harambee schools' committees and information

text. Government is now worried about the spread of Harambee schools and especially about political competition over the schools and proliferation of them through "leaders' " competition to get their own schools started. Before Harambee schools are allowed to start, often a large deposit must be made so that teachers' salaries can be covered. This is a rule of the Ministry of Education. Officers of that Ministry in the districts spend a good deal of time on the unaided school question. They are pressured to recommend that Government take over Harambee Schools. Community development officers have also been told to try to control the spread of the schools. And provincial planning officers have had as their main mission a rationalization of self-help projects as well as the locating of new African businesses and trading depots. If local, district, and even national political leaders become involved in pressuring the representatives of the central ministries or intervene at the central level, then the provincial administration invariably comes into play.

After spending much time and effort promulgating the idea of local participation in self-help and Harambee schools, provincial and district commissioners now must act to control spontaneous activities. Yet there are costs in trying to limit the strong self-help drive. There is political reaction against it and it risks curtailing local economic initiatives. Moreover, some provincial administrators and community development officers are themselves highly sympathetic to the self-help drive. Provincial planning officers sometimes see their Civil Service colleagues as naive about development and as part of

---

about Government came from veterinary and agricultural officers and officials in the provincial administration.

the problem of rational planning when they refuse to try to channel or stem the flow of social service demands.[54] What the Harambee school issue above all illustrates is that for important parts of Kenya the problem is not one of mobilizing people to want more or to invest time and money in self-improvement. Moreover, the investment in time and money for schooling cuts across poorer and better-off farmers and cuts across ethnic lines although it is most evident in Kikuyu areas. The present regime, after first fostering local participation around the building of Harambee schools is now nervous about the consequences for its budget. Yet it is sensitive to the pressures to take over unaided schools and concerned about the cycle of education, migration, and unemployment in the towns. It has preferred local participation through concrete self-help projects to participation in competitive politics expressed electorally. Of course, politics still gets expressed through the local projects.

The Kenyan regime appears correct in thinking it knows what large numbers of people want without having to have a strong party organization channeling demands upward. The problem for Government is not mobilizing people in the central core areas through exhortation and organizational means. Government's problem is in handling local demands which may be parochial from its point of view. It wants to control the demands without creating political opposition or communal apathy. It also has a problem in that many demands and pressures come from the ethnic group which is its major support—Kikuyus—and thus are seen as threatening by other ethnic groups.

[54] From interviews with planning officers, provincial administrators, and provincial trade officers in 1968-69.

D. THE CIVIL SERVICE AS A CLASS?

I have argued that Government hopes to control and channel demands through its Civil Service. We should return briefly to a critique of the Civil Service more fundamental perhaps than the question of whether it is the institution best suited to developmental tasks.

The aforementioned Commission of Inquiry on the public service from time to time alluded to fundamental problems of accountability of the Civil Service and the matter of civil servants' private rather than public behavior. One of the main tasks was to consider whether Civil Service remuneration made sense in the light of cost of living, market pressures, growth of GDP, and the capacity of the country to meet costs of possible increases —all in the context of income distribution between persons and regions.[55] The conclusion reached by the Commission was that an increase in wages of public sector employees was unavoidable because of pressures built up during the last few years. However, the Commission recommended that public sector wage increases should be accompanied by an intensification of existing Government policies for rural development; a policy which should reverse the internal terms of trade that have been increasingly unfavorable to farmers. It also recommended changes in the tax system so that more labor-intensive technologies would be encouraged.[56]

More frontal assaults have been made on the Civil Service which have shared the Commission's concern for rural development but which have also described both civil servants and politicians as parasites living off the peasantry. Indeed, critics of urban-based elites have

[55] Ndegwa Commission, *op.cit.*, p. 26.
[56] *Ibid.*, p. 44.

argued that tensions between civil servants and politicians obscure the class interest that they both share, as opposed to rural people. In Kenya, the argument has been made that the top Government leaders have taken power from the National Assembly and given it to civil servants and that the administrative officers have in general assumed the role of party. This argument has been made by MPs and unhappy middle-level KANU officials.[57] Others would go even further and argue that the basic cleavage is between the "haves" and "have nots" in Kenya and Africa as a whole and that middle-level KANU politicians and anyone with a wage income is a "have."

A deliberately balanced view of the Kenya Civil Service would have to include positive aspects: the Governmental system has remained relatively stable, the Kenya bureaucracy spreads the authority of the state through the countryside; at the least it has not hindered respectable economic growth.[58] Moreover, the Kenya Civil Service delivers real services. Taxes are collected by the provincial administration; Kenya has the broadest agricultural extension service in Africa. It would be very hard to measure how high the cost of these services is to society as a whole either in their specifics or in the aggregate.[59] Moreover, while Kenya has had a strong Civil

[57] See for example the remarks of M. Seroney, an MP in *East African Standard* (Nairobi) March 18, 1971. Even the National Executive Officer of KANU asserted that KANU was dead and that administrative officers in the provincial administration had taken over. *East African Standard*, March 18, 1971, as cited by Nellis, in *Is the Kenyan Bureaucracy Developmental?*

[58] See Nellis, *Who Pays Taxes in Kenya?* and Ndegwa Commission, *op.cit.*, p. 398.

[59] Nellis, in *op.cit.*, has questioned whether the provincial administration collection of graduated personal tax amounts to a net gain in Kenya. Hans Ruthenberg, *African Agricultural Pro-*

Service by African standards, it is given great tasks. Even if one should decide that the Kenyan Civil Service is swollen in terms of Kenya's budget, the Civil Service operates out of weakness in terms of low ratios of personnel to total population, and where in general the state is highly constrained in its ability to intervene in economic and social life.[60]

The argument that a bureaucratic-executive alliance exists in Kenya must be taken seriously but it seems questionable that we can treat the Kenyan Civil Service exclusively or even largely in class terms, although it is obviously a privileged group in Kenya.[61] Okumu has seen this alliance in terms of a convergence of interests among members of a new middle class. Conflicts which might arise between the Civil Service and other structures, he says, are mediated by the basic convergence of

---

duction: Development Policy in Kenya, 1952-1965 (Berlin: Springer-Verlag, 1966) has argued that Kenya cannot support the high cost of its agricultural extension network. Moris, in "Agrarian Revolution," states a similar view.

[60] Bienen, "Economic Environment." Also see Guy Hunter, "Development Administration in East Africa," *Journal of Administration Overseas*, Vol. 6, No. 1 (January 1967), p. 12. Hunter notes that as of the mid-1960s, in Kenya the ratio of agricultural extension workers to farming units was 1:700. In Holland it was 1:250, with a much more densely settled population and easier transportation.

[61] The debates about the usefulness of seeing institutions in class terms are many. See Manfred Halpern, *The Politics of Social Change in North Africa and the Middle East* (Princeton: Princeton University Press, 1963); Milovan Djilas, *The New Class* (New York: Frederick Praeger, 1957); Jose Nun, "The Middle-Class Coup," in Claudio Veliz, ed., *The Politics of Conformity* (London: Oxford University Press, 1967).

interest between civil servants, politicians and other members of the middle class.[62]

The Civil Service is a strategic interest group, but is it a group with special norms? It is recruited from particular ethnic as well as social communities. Its members define their own social and economic interests and the ways they do this affect the ways that the Civil Service functions as a mechanism for control, development, and participation. But it is a mistake to consider it in uniform corporate or institutional terms any more than class ones. Thus different functional categories within the Civil Service are more or less interested in local participation or in control over it. Community development officers and field officers of the provincial administration find themselves with different constituencies and having to do different things to succeed in terms of the goals set for them and which they set for themselves. Levels of the bureaucracy must also be distinguished. Nellis observes that the leading politicians and civil servants support the notion of rural development and that divisional civil servants and local politicians are active in rural improvement but that the mass of bureaucrats in between seem indifferent.[63] Moreover, the Civil Service must be distinguished by age and rank as well. Its splits do not simply mirror those of society nor can it be posed as a categorical group vis-à-vis society.

For certain purposes the Civil Service may be distinguished from the rest of society by income and educational standards. But within the Civil Service, fissures

[62] Okumu, "The Socio-Political Setting."

[63] John Nellis, "The Administration of Rural Development in Kenya," *East African Journal*, Vol. 9, No. 3 (March 1972), p. 15.

appear by function and tribe and grade and level of operation. So far, the political goals set for Kenya by its present leadership have usually coincided with bureaucratic ones in that order and stability have been stressed. The way that the politicians have frequently defined development has often meant administration—getting things done, establishing administrative networks. However, relations with politicians are variable. At the senior levels, ministers resemble senior civil servants more than other politicians by education and income. But senior civil servants are more production-oriented while senior politicians have been responsive to welfare demands. (President Kenyatta on one occasion opted for free out-patient care without consultation with his senior civil servants in the Ministry of Health.)

Politicians have been reluctant to try to stem demands. At the local level, civil servants are given the job of trying to rationalize demands and are not allocated enough resources to accommodate demands. Thus it is at this level that tensions between politicians and civil servants appear clearly. Civil servants will complain that MPs do not involve themselves in local matters and in the next breath say that it is a good thing they do not. When district development advisory committees were set up which were meant to bring together civil servants and political and associational group representatives, civil servants often saw the articulation of demands as a stirring up of land problems or cooperative movement problems. Sometimes district commissioners would attend county council meetings and be received hostilely. At the same time, civil servants will also want to show that "something is being done" in their areas and will press local demands upward, getting into difficulties with bureaucrats in control who have supervisory or integrating roles, e.g., planning officers. The planning officers will see other civil servants as becoming political people. It is not surprising that planning officers and outside observers will often decry the difficulty of getting local officials, not to say ordinary citizens, "meaningfully involved" in producing integrated programs or plans. What has emerged from attempts to involve local officials and citizens in grass-roots planning are shopping lists of projects wanted.[64] Planning officers get the injunctions to involve local people and administrative machinery for participation is proliferated, but at the same time, the center wants "sensible" and integrated plans to flow upward.[65]

The picture I have sketched so far is one in which Civil Service plays a major role and the society is one with many local associations, self-help units, and strong demands made on central resources.

I have argued that the Civil Service is given the task of channeling these demands and at the same time is the critical institution of social control. By virtue of being the agent for social control in Kenya, the Civil Service is involved frequently in curtailing political participation. When economic and social demands cannot be met, the Civil Service is given the mission of restricting political

[64] Nellis, *ibid.*, implies that meaningful involvement has not taken place when this occurs.

[65] For a discussion of this in Tanzania see Bienen, *Tanzania*, pp. 281-333. In Kenya, the Ministry of Economic Planning and Development established an array of administrative structures to get coordination and participation in the late 1960s as Tanzania had done five years earlier. Nairobi, according to Nellis, wanted the planning exercise to be as decentralized as possible, "but the fulcrum of the operation tended to be located between the provincial planning officer and the district development committee" (other civil servants). Nellis, "Administration of Rural Development," p. 12.

formations which push these demands upward. Or when political competition itself threatens stability, the Civil Service imposes limits on it. At the same time, the Civil Service itself pushes demands upward as it communicates grievances from below. The Civil Service gives influence to demands by organizing them for those who become constituents. Members of the provincial administration find themselves doing this as well as officials of the central ministries. Frequently, the civil servants are the only ones in Kenya who can organize demands for people in the rural areas and make them felt at higher levels. The Civil Service becomes a vehicle for political participation as it communicates views and makes rural interests felt at the center through its mechanisms. There is a great sensitivity of the center to rural demands and there is often a congruence between goals of the center and the localities. This is established through the Civil Service which provides information to the center, organizes demands, and funnels benefits downward.

So far, I have concentrated on the role of the Civil Service in coming to grips with interests and demands from below in rural areas. We shall see that it also becomes the focus for demands from middle- and high-level elites who want loans, land benefits, licenses. Since these elites can bring to bear individual influence and better organization of their interests, their relationship to the Civil Service is more clearly one of political reciprocity.

At all levels in Kenya, people must react to the Civil Service. They must deal with it or try to avoid it. The Civil Service is thrust into the political realm also because of the fragmented nature of party in Kenya and because of the relationship of President Kenyatta to KANU. We can see the Civil Service operate in the political process as it tries to control and respond to overtly political interests by looking at elections and party factions. A discussion of party politics is necessary for understanding elite participation in politics.

III

Describing Kenya: Party Politics

A. PARTY COMPETITION

Just as commentators on the Kenya scene have stressed the strength of the Civil Service and the provincial administration in particular, they have invariably noted the weakness of party and the fragmentation of KANU in Kenyan political life. Discussions of KANU have stressed its inability to frame policy or to function as a channel of demands upward or orders downward. Indeed, politicians, civil servants, social scientists have gone so far as to deny KANU any meaningful role in Kenya or even to attribute to it an existence beyond a nominal one.

If KANU has no political meaning, we must ask: why do some individuals invest time and money and energy competing for its posts at national and local levels? Moreover, we must also try to assess the consequences of party politics for the ways that demands are structured and political competition takes place. I argue below that KANU does provide an arena of competition in Kenya. It does provide a vehicle for participation for at least some people. And even if we should determine that KANU itself is moribund in many respects, we must see how this matters for participation.

The first thing to note is that Kenya is still nominally ruled by a party. This is not the case in a host of African countries where militaries have carried out successful coups and ended party rule once or more than once.[1] Moreover, KANU remains a dominant party. That is, party opposition has been consistently driven out of existence in Kenya, although not always by electoral competition alone. Administrative means have been wielded against the opposition parties. Government has at times refused to let opposition candidates contest seats, banned the KPU, and jailed opposition leaders. Yet Kenya has not become a *de jure* one-party state as has Tanzania. And KANU has shown a capacity to be absorptive. That is, opposition has been coopted or intimidated back into KANU. Various leaders of all opposition parties have one time or another come back into KANU.

Originally, party competition was between KANU and KADU. Kenya's first general election in February 1961 was contested between the two parties. KADU polled only 16.4 percent of the votes, yet some of its candidates won over 90 percent of the votes in Nandi and Kipsigis districts in the Rift Valley and in some coastal districts.[2] In a 1963 election, KADU was able to retain its hold on the minority tribes' allegiances through its own loose alliance system of factional leaders. Thus Kalenjin, some Luhya, Masai, and Coastal (Mijikenda) tribes continued to vote for KADU. When KADU leaders crossed the

[1] For a discussion of military intervention in Africa see among others: Claude Welch, ed., *Soldier and State in Africa* (Evanston: Northwestern University Press, 1970); Henry Bienen, ed., *The Military Intervenes: Case Studies in Political Development* (New York: Russell Sage Foundation, 1968); Ruth First, *Power in Africa* (New York: Pantheon, 1970); Ernest W. Lefever, *Spear and Scepter* (Washington: The Brookings Institution, 1970).

[2] Bennett and Rosberg, *op.cit.*, p. 185 and *passim*.

floor in 1964 to join KANU, prominent oppositionists became KANU Government Cabinet leaders. Thus Daniel Arap Moi, a KADU leader, is now Kenya's Vice President. Ronald Ngala, a Coastal leader, has been a Cabinet member. The 1963 election saw the creation of another tribally based party, The African Peoples Party. APP was a vehicle for the Kamba leader Paul Ngei. Because he did not receive the national power and status he wanted from KANU leaders, and because other KANU leaders were to form factional groups with Kamba leaders who opposed Ngei in his own home area, Ngei broke away and formed his own party. In the May 1963 general elections, Ngei's APP polled over 104,548 votes in six Lower House seats in the Machakos Districts of Ukambani to 6,935 for KANU and 12,090 for four independents.[3] Ngei, too was absorbed into KANU and became first the head of an important statutory board and then a Minister.

There were two strong impetuses to this early pattern of ingestion into KANU. Opposition was tribally based and thus not easily removed. A dominant alliance of tribes could prevail but it could not obliterate opposition. Consequently, attempts were made to bring dissident leaders into KANU. This was possible since oppositions were not fundamentally rooted in policy differences nor in deep social cleavages but in ethnic competition for

[3] For a discussion of the APP and the 1963 election in general see Clyde Sanger and John Nottingham, "The Kenya General Election of 1963," *The Journal of Modern African Studies*, Vol. 2, No. 1 (1964), pp. 1-40. After a system of National Members bonus seats was applied, KANU had 83 seats, KADU had 33, and the APP had 8 in the Lower House. In the Senate it was 20, 16, and 2 respectively as KADU was better able to translate its support from minority tribes into Senate than House seats.

spoils. A group could be "brought in" by bringing in its leaders.

The other impetus for bringing blocs into KANU was the internal competition within that party itself. As KANU leaders fought with each other at the center they sought to make alliances into each other's district territory and also with those outside of KANU. Opponents of Odinga in KANU hoped to strengthen themselves by bringing in KADU leaders. When the former leaders of KADU came into KANU, the Odinga wing of KANU became increasingly isolated. At a critical KANU conference held in Limuru in 1966, it became clear that opponents of the ruling KANU group could be defeated with the aid of former KADU opponents.

One consequence of this pattern of fusion and bringing in contending groups was the concomitant development of patterns of fission. Groups who became isolated in KANU split off. The fission-fusion pattern can be seen with the emergence, and then elimination, of the major opposition party to KANU, the KPU.[4]

Oginga Odinga resigned his KANU Vice Presidency after he was clearly out-maneuvered at the Limuru conference and soon became KPU leader. The KPU was less of a congeries of district and tribal alliances than KADU had been. The KPU had a solid Luo base in the Nyanza Districts of Kenya and received support from Luo in Nairobi and in the other major towns where they worked, especially Mombasa. Splits within KANU itself and factionalism within Kikuyu areas gave the KPU some wedge in non-Luo areas. The KPU tried to extend itself beyond

---

[4] A valuable study of the KPU is Susanne Mueller, "Political Parties in Kenya: The Politics of Opposition and Dissent 1919-1969," Ph.D. thesis submitted to the Department of Politics, Princeton University, 1972.

its Luo constituency by appealing to urban and agricultural workers and to landless elements. The Kikuyu leader Kaggia became deputy head of the KPU and his appeal was explicitly to poorer Kikuyu; moreover, he represented a pan-tribal appeal and personified the KPU's attempt to create a class party.

There were and are great difficulties in creating a class-based organization which would reach out to student elites and to marginals—landless, unemployed—and at the same time reach out to workers. In Kenya, unionized workers are already a labor aristocracy and have not been ready allies for recent migrants to cities and the rural and urban unemployed or student elites. Also, the KPU itself depended heavily on the personal positions of Kaggia and Odinga and this boded ill for creating a nonpersonalistic, class-based party.

Still, the KPU could not be defeated by KANU in its own Luo strongholds. Odinga and thirty other MPS resigned in April 1966, and constitutional changes were made immediately following the resignations, forcing them to stand again in by-elections. This resulted in the so-called Little General Election of 1966.[5] The KPU contested 28

[5] When the KANU majority passed retroactive legislation making MPS who changed parties contest new by-elections, MPS who had announced that they would join the KPU were told that they could remain in KANU if they renounced their switch to the KPU. A number did so but were made to contest the by-elections anyway. The Kenya pattern of reincorporation into KANU has never been based on good will toward opponents. It was not a live and let live attitude which governed but a necessity of politics stemming from the recognition of internal KANU divisions and ethnic-district fragmentation in Kenya. For a discussion of the Little General Election of 1966 see Gertzel, *The Politics of Independent Kenya*, pp. 73-124; John Harbeson, "The Kenya Little General Election: A Study in Problems of Urban Political Integra-

of the 29 seats which were fought. KANU won 21 Lower House seats to the KPU's 7 and KANU won 8 Senate seats to the KPU's 2. But in the Nyanza or Luo areas where the KPU did win, the majorities were massive. This pattern was reproduced again in 1969 when a by-election was fought in a Nyanza constituency called Gem where a KPU candidate again overwhelmingly defeated the KANU candidate.[6] Similarly, in a number of rural areas where KANU was strong, it won overwhelmingly. There were elections, however, which were more competitive. These were either in mixed ethnic areas or in swing areas, that is, areas where the ethnic groups were not clearly committed to the dominant KANU coalition based on massive Kikuyu support. Kamba, Teso, and Luhya areas were such and they continued to have internal factionalism which the competing parties tried to exploit.

The Government refused to allow contested municipal elections to take place in 1968 when the KPU would have challenged KANU in many towns. It also had banned the KPU by the time the first general election since 1963 was held in December 1969. At that time, some KPU leaders were in detention. But the pattern of taking opposition into or back into KANU prevailed. Kaggia, the deputy leader of the KPU, had come back into KANU before the December election and was allowed to stand in the general election even though it was a primary

tion," IDS Discussion Paper No. 52, Nairobi, June 1967; David Koff, "Kenya's Little General Election," *Africa Report*, Vol. 11, No. 7 (October 1966), pp. 57-60; George Bennett, "Kenya's Little General Election," *World Today*, Vol. 22, No. 8 (August 1966), pp. 336-343.

[6] See John Okumu, "The By-Election in Gem," *East Africa Journal*, Vol. 6, No. 8 (June 1969), pp. 9-17.

election where KANU membership was required.[7] Prior to his detention, Odinga was frequently asked to rejoin KANU and he did so in September 1971, some time after his release from detention. A former KPU leader, Dennis Akumu, became for a time head of the central trade union organization. Thus the rise and end of the KPU did not represent deviance from the basic Kenya pattern. Indeed, that pattern depended more on KANU's own organization and social base, which in turn reflected many of the facts of Kenyan life that gave rise to opposition parties.

KANU itself had various ethnic bases and was vulnerable to ethnic-based appeals. KANU was not a mass-based party that could mobilize large numbers of voters to the polls and in which power and authority were concentrated in the party's central executive institution. Early writings on KANU stressed that KANU's objective was the organization of a mass movement and that it could be distinguished from the opposition KADU by its dynamism and by KADU's reliance on tribal and regional associations.[8] Yet Rosberg and Bennett who made this comparison between KANU and KADU noted that "from the moment of its establishment KANU was unable to achieve its aspirations and intentions of building an all-embracing centralized and unitary type of mass party."[9] And they

[7] The legislation establishing the 1969 primary required KANU membership for six months before a candidate could stand. Exceptions were made for some civil servants and for Grace Onyango, an important Luo leader and KPU leader and for Kaggia, former Deputy Chairman of the KPU.

[8] Rosberg and Bennett, *op.cit.*, p. 27.

[9] *Ibid.*, pp. 41-42. Implicitly, KANU was being compared to what, in the early 1960s, were thought of as strong mass mobilization parties, e.g., TANU in Tanganyika, the Convention Peoples Party in Ghana. For a "revisionist" analysis of African one-

focused their analysis on two important reasons why KANU never advanced beyond a confederal type of political organization: the leadership problem and the district base of power in KANU politics.

B. LEADERSHIP IN KENYA

Many African countries came to independence with a party that had once been a national movement which had led the anti-colonial struggle. This national movement become party was often identified with a strong leader whose activities were frequently analyzed in terms of the concept of charisma. David Apter started this when he saw Nkrumah's role in Ghana as an attempt to transfer traditional loyalties into the personal allegiances to him preparatory to transferring them to a new set of institutions.[10] Others used the notion of charisma more loosely than Apter and applied it to any strong leader who dominated his party or who cast a large shadow. More recently, African leaders have been portrayed more as bosses than as charismatic figures.[11]

The importance of personal leadership in Africa, whether that leadership be understood as charismatic, or more properly understood, I think, as leadership of a personal, political-machine type or patrimonial-traditional type, or combinations of the two types,[12] has been the

---

party systems see Aristide Zolberg, *Creating Political Order*; Bienen, *Tanzania*; Bienen, "African One-Party Systems."

[10] David Apter, *Ghana in Transition.*

[11] For a discussion of Nkrumah as a political boss see Henry Bretton, *The Rise and Fall of Kwame Nkrumah* (New York, Praeger, 1966). For a general discussion see Zolberg, *op.cit.* and Bienen, "One Party Systems in Africa."

[12] Gruenther Roth, "Personal Rulership, Patrimonialism and Empire-building in the New States," *World Politics*, Vol. 20,

other side of the coin of institutional weakness and decentralization. Personal machines can be centralized and they certainly can be tough and coercive as a number of American machines were. In the African context, however, personal leadership has been usually a substitute for effective institutions, and not a very good substitute even from the point of view of leaders themselves. And personal leadership has proved to be rather fragile with some few exceptions. Haile Selassie gets high marks for durability in a patrimonial system; Julius Nyerere has tried to institutionalize a party with some success. Felix Houphet-Boigny has ruled through a political party in eminently good "boss" style. Jomo Kenyatta has ruled above party, by manipulating factions, working through a relatively strong Civil Service, operating in a rather narrow sphere of concerns, utilizing his ethnic base but at the same time appealing to all Kenyans with the force of his historical position as "He who suffered for the Kenyan Nation," as the spokesman for Kenyan nationalism, as the Mzee or Elder of the nation.

Jomo Kenyatta has been a famous African leader. But for all his fame, Kenyatta has not been thought of either within or outside of Kenya as a dynamic leader who has equated himself with party and nation. Kenyatta had not brought the nation to independence via a political organization he dominated, as did, for example, Nyerere in Tanzania, Nkrumah in Ghana, Keita in Mali, Houphet-Boigny in Ivory Coast, Toure in Guinea. Kenyatta was

No. 2 (January 1968), pp. 194-206, has elaborated on the concept of patrimonialism as applied to new states. He distinguishes two kinds of patrimonialism: the historical survival of traditional patrimonial regimes and personal rulership linked to material rewards and incentives. I call the latter type machine politics and reserve the use of patrimonial for Roth's first type.

in jail while the major parties were forming in Kenya. He emerged as a critical force in the negotiations for independence as the lines were drawn between ethnic groups and personal factions. His role, however, was not analogous to that of leaders who had forged political parties and surrounded them with ideologies of development. While Kenyatta was a political force, he was not a constant factor in organization building in Kenya. He appeared to many observers to be above the fray and almost above politics. Indeed, Kenyatta was not always taken seriously as a political leader whose style and preferences were important for Kenyan political life.[13]

Kenyatta has been a difficult political figure for observers to understand because much of his activity in politics is of the court variety. He is certainly visible in Kenya in that he makes speeches to large crowds, travels in motorcades, hosts visiting delegations of foreigners and delegations of Kenyans who come to State House or to his home in Gatundu to pay homage. Kenyatta's activities are widely reported on the radio. Kenyans learn that Mzee Kenyatta has gone to the Coast for a vacation or received, yet again, traditional dancers at his home. But the visibility is that of a monarch; he is seen at a distance. He is reported on but what he knows and thinks is not widely known. Thus it has been hard to identify Kenyatta either with specific social and economic policies or with particular political positions. Kenyatta holds sway at his home in Gatundu and Ministers and others come to him there to petition for favors. Blood ties to

[13] One exception is John Okumu, "Charisma and Politics," pp. 9-16. Two autobiographies of major Kenyan political leaders never confront the role of Kenyatta head on. See Odinga, *op.cit.*, and Kaggia, *op.cit.*

him have been important for one's advancement.[14] Individuals personally connected to Kenyatta but not necessarily widely known in Kenya or abroad may become important at certain points in time.[15] The politics of family ties and intrigue at the court is a hard politics to analyze in its particulars. But we can state some of its consequences. Policy matters are not openly debated. Clan ties and ties of locale are important and a politics which starts from blood connections can become patrimonial.[16] Kenyatta has never equated party and state as Nkrumah did in Ghana. He has been accused of treating the state as a family possession. The head of the family

[14] Kenyatta and Mbiyu Koinange, an important Minister, are brothers by marriage. Njoroge Mungai, at different times Minister for Defense and Foreign Affairs is a close cousin and had been married to a sister of James Gichuru, another important Minister. Appolo Njonjo, "Kenya: The Problem of Succession and the Issues Behind the Plot," unpublished paper, Princeton, 1971.

[15] Various personal secretaries of Kenyatta have been important. Some of them have become public figures. Njonjo, *op.cit.* points to the importance of Arthur Wanyoike during the period when Kikuyu oathing took place at Gatundu after Tom Mboya's assassination.

[16] The inner core of Kenyatta's Cabinet has been not only Kikuyu but from a particular area, the home area of Kenyatta-Kiambu. Kenyatta has also been open to the accusation that he has used public means for private accumulation. He seems to have shared the view of many who suffered—i.e., that they would use public means to reconstitute their lives and fortunes. Politics became highly personalized for many Kikuyu after suffering for the common cause. Kenyatta has also told MPs that in office they had had their chance to do something for themselves and he once reproached Kaggia for not having done something for himself in business or farming while in public office.

is aged, however, so internal factionalism becomes inextricably bound up with the politics of succession.[17]

Nonetheless, Kenyatta has not ruled by clique alone. He has ruled through a Civil Service he inherited and which was a more docile instrument than party. Some see Kenyatta as the last of the colonial Governors because of his choice of the Civil Service. But the Civil Service was the only instrument available to Kenyatta. He could Africanize it at the top with individuals loyal to him. Some Europeans who felt at the time of independence that Kenyatta would be too weak to control other leaders in KANU just as he had been too weak in 1950-52 to control militants in the Kenya Africa Union (KAU) failed to consider that this time Kenyatta had a Government machinery at his disposal.[18]

[17] For a discussion of the succession in Kenya see Njonjo, *op.cit.*, and John Murray, "Succession Prospects in Kenya," *Africa Report*, Vol. 13, No. 8 (November 1968), pp. 44-48. Not all the inner circle around Kenyatta have had their own political bases. Charles Njonjo, long-time Attorney General, does not. Not all would agree on who constitutes the "inner core." It is the nature of court politics that such matters are uncertain, perhaps even to the participants themselves, and that the leader who manipulates his coteries should deliberately make it so.

[18] Some Europeans at the time of Mau Mau saw Kenyatta as "the leader unto darkness and death." Others saw him as an impotent figure. In Kaggia's own memoirs it is stated that Kenyatta was never a Mau Mau leader and that he was warned by Mau Mau that he was making too strong anti-Mau Mau statements under orders from the colonial regime. While he was portrayed as the Mau Mau leader by the colonial regime, Kenyatta always denied it. After he came out of prison he was faced by continued opposition from ex-detainees and forest fighters who had remained in the forests and he was extremely tough with them. An official editing of his speeches and experiences published in 1968 heavily stressed Kenyatta's opposition to Mau Mau violence both in historical retrospect and currently.

Kenyatta has been accused of neglecting the alternative of party building.[19] But the option of control through KANU was not open to him. Kenyatta was imprisoned after the famous Kapenguria trial. He remained in prison, often under conditions of extreme hardship when he was already at an advanced age, from 1953 until 1961. It was the period of imprisonment which solidified Kenyatta's hold on Kenya Africans, but it also removed him from operative control of any political organization in the critical formative period of parties in Kenya.[20] Kenyatta had never been unassailable within the old KAU. He was challenged in it by younger leaders, Kaggia especially. As Kenyatta's detention was coming to an end, younger leaders who had emerged in the 1950s were not eager to give way. Kenyatta may even have thought that some of these younger leaders, Mboya in particular, had col-

---

See Jomo Kenyatta, *Suffering Without Bitterness* (Nairobi: East African Publishing House, 1968), esp. pp. 21-26. When Kenyatta came out of prison, he called for reconciliation among Kenyans who had opposed each other during Mau Mau. This was a call for reconciliation between European and Africans. But above all, it was a call for reconciliation among Kikuyu who had opposed each other.

[19] Okumu, "Charisma and Politics," and also "The Problem of Party Leadership in Kenya: Notes and Comments," unpublished paper, University of East Africa, Social Science Conference, January 1968.

[20] It is an irony of history that Kenyatta was to be offered chairmanship of three parties he showed relatively little interest in. In detention, the detainees Kaggia, Fred Kubai, Paul Ngei, and Kunga Karumba had formed a party, the National Democratic Party, replete with symbols, flag, and constitution. Kenyatta was made its head although he seemed to have little interest in it. He was offered the chairmanship of KADU, which he refused, and he then accepted KANU's chairmanship.

luded to keep him in detention.[21] Soon after his release, Kenyatta tried to undermine Mboya's trade union base. Much of Odinga's ascendance until 1965 can be seen as an attempt by Kenyatta and those around him to strike at Mboya as the most dangerous of the would-be challengers. When Odinga's own power grew too great, Kenyatta out-maneuvered him and his allies and then openly opposed the left in KANU.[22]

[21] Bennett and Rosberg, *op.cit.*, pp. 131-133.

[22] Mboya was the most able and vigorous of the young Ministers and party leaders and one most widely connected throughout Kenya—by virtue of his trade union base and his functioning as Secretary General of KANU. He was also by upbringing a man who had lived in many different worlds. He was Luo by birth but also lived in Kamba and Kikuyu areas and could speak these languages as well as Swahili and English. Neither Mboya nor Odinga, however, had strong Kikuyu bases although Mboya had won his seat in Parliament in a Nairobi constituency with many Kikuyu and his own early party had been a pan-tribal one. In some respects, the most dangerous challenger for Kenyatta in the past was Kaggia because he had deep Kikuyu roots, had suffered in prison with Kenyatta, and also had ties outside his home area. He served as KANU district chairman for a time in Naivasha in the Rift Valley, a mixed Kikuyu and non-Kikuyu area, and he made non-tribal appeals for support based on programs which challenged the regime's own. In the 1966 Little General Election, it was Kaggia that Kenyatta campaigned directly against in Kandara constituency. He did not throw his weight in other constituencies. The breach between them had been evident as early as 1963 when Kenyatta pressured for Kaggia's resignation as Assistant Minister from his Government. Their poor relations go back to pre-Mau Mau days when Kaggia took a much more militant anti-colonial stand. Their relations in prison, when they spent years together at Lodwar in northern Kenya, were not good. Odinga deferred much more to Kenyatta and Kenyatta was more reluctant to break with Odinga which meant a break with at least a large share of Luos in Kenya,

It was, of course, to Kenyatta's advantage not to become openly enmeshed in factional fighting in KANU if he could avoid it. Leaders would come away from meetings with him thinking he had accepted their position only to find out to the contrary. Kenyatta did take sides in KANU politics and he would throw the weight of the Civil Service to one side or another by allowing a particular faction to be registered as *the* KANU branch for a district or town. But he tried to cast himself in the role of arbitrator above the fray.

It has been Kenyatta's genius to perceive that he could maintain his position in Kenya only by avoiding KANU as an institution of rule. He would exhort the party and try to destroy contending parties. But Kenyatta never appears to have taken seriously the prospect of ruling through the party rather than through his governmental apparatus, despite injunctions to KANU to be better organized and disciplined.[23] To get involved in KANU politics would mean vying with individuals in their own bailiwicks and possibly losing at the district levels. Kenyatta intervened in extreme circumstances and on some of these occasions there had already been violence in internal KANU fighting. This occurred in Mombasa and Machakos. Then Kenyatta suspended party activity in the district involved. Usually, Kenyatta let factional politics take its course in the districts or he let his lieutenants at the center line up with various factions.

By not involving himself openly in factional politics, Kenyatta could be seen as *the* Kenyan leader. If other leaders tried to use Kenyatta for their own purposes in

Odinga acted in Kenyatta's name prior to the open break in a way Kaggia never had.

[23] See Kenyatta, "The Party Dynamic," in *Suffering Without Bitterness*, pp. 298-301.

internal struggles, it is clear that Kenyatta used them and that he played this game best of all. Kenyatta grew into his own myth. That is, he became untouchable in Kenyan politics by being elevated by his lieutenants and by fulfilling their need for a unifier within KANU and in Kenya more generally. If, as Njonjo states, the cult of Kenyatta arose out of the need of other leaders to invent a neutral unifying symbol for a faction-ridden movement, Kenyatta used these needs himself.[24]

Kenyatta's major use of KANU has been as an arena in which to let others struggle for control of subsidiary resources. He has had no clear commitment to it and he has rarely invested his personal prestige in its doings.[25] He has certainly never devolved power to it.

To have done so would have been tantamount to giving up central rule to the district and subdistrict KANU organizations. For unlike TANU in Tanzania which had local roots and also a national center, KANU was weak at the center and frequently did not have grassroots organization. It has been a party of the middle, of notables and district, municipal, town elites who have contended with each other in the many arenas Kenya provided: county councils, regional assemblies until they were abolished, KANU district and town branches, cooperatives, Harambee school committees, ethnic and religious associations.

C. KANU OF THE DISTRICTS

Kanu has been characterized by the absence of strong central institutions and by the district and constituency

[24] Njonjo, *op.cit.*

[25] Kenneth Good, "Kenyatta and the Organization of KANU," *Canadian Journal of African Studies*, Vol. II, No. 2 (1968), p. 132.

base of its politics and by its open internal factionalism. Because KANU's central institutions are weak and the party fails to operate in accord with its own constitutional provisions for elections of party officials and convening of party conferences and councils,[26] there has been a tendency to dismiss party in Kenya. It is true that the Cabinet, Parliament, and the Civil Service were all dominated by an inner governmental executive while KANU's Governing Council and National Executive atrophied. It is also true that KANU was and is faction ridden and that the central KANU institutions have not functioned to make policy. National personnel changes are made without reference to party bodies. However, it would not be accurate to call Kenya a no-party state. Just as by deduction we should have earlier known that the so-called mass-mobilization parties could not penetrate the rural African countryside in ways alleged by commentators in the early 1960s, we should stop and pause to consider that the very vigorous factionalism within KANU

[26] The KANU Constitution called for an annual delegates' conference every year but until a conference was called at Limuru in March 1966 there had been none since 1962. There are various versions of the KANU Constitution. The ones I have seen are mimeographed; it is interesting that KANU has never widely circulated printed versions of its own Constitution. Nor do versions exist in every major tribal language. The earliest version of the KANU Constitution called for the All-Union Executive Committee having the power to convene conferences at quarterly intervals as directed or recommended by the Supreme Council of the Union. The later ones referred to the National Executive Committee convening an August conference every year. These Constitutions are not dated. For a discussion of KANU's failure to comply with Constitutional Provisions on finances, meetings, suspension of members, and nominations, see Taita Towet, "KANU: the Neglected Constitution," *Kenya Weekly News* (Nakuru), April 18, 1969, p. 8.

and the struggle over party posts means that for at least some people KANU is an arena worth contending in. In various districts KANU is an important resource for middle-level leaders as they contend for power. One should not jump to the conclusion that because a Civil Service is relatively strong and policy making is tightly controlled by a small group around the President that a party has no meaning.[27] We have to establish what meanings KANU has for various groups and what the consequences of specific factional patterns are.

We can say, however, that the KANU Constitution's assertion that "K.A.N.U. will govern the country through the established structure of the civil service, and administration" and that "K.A.N.U.'s policies will be reflected and implemented in the actions, administrations, and policies of the country through the decision of the Cabinet, Parliament, and the establishment of the necessary machinery for consultation and cooperation between the party, the public and the government" is true only in the formal sense that KANU forms the Government with its parliamentary majority. Yet the majority within Parliament, even when the KADU and KPU were operating, was kept together by virtue of President Kenyatta's own authority and the operation of a reward system for Ministers, Assistant Ministers, and backbenchers alike. These rewards were channeled through the President's Office or through Ministries which gave individuals appoint-

[27] For a discussion of the no-party state argument see Immanual Wallerstein, "The Decline of the Party in Single Party States," in Weiner and LaPalombara, *Political Parties and Political Development,* pp. 201-216; and Robert Rotberg, "Modern African Studies: Problems and Prospects," *World Politics,* Vol. 18, No. 3 (April 1966), pp. 365-578. My own discussion of the subject can be found in Bienen, "One-Party Systems in Africa," pp. 109-110.

ments to statutory boards. In a study of the Kenya Parliament, Jay Hakes argues that the KANU Parliamentary Party behaves, by and large, in a cohesive way but that neither national nor district party organizations were determinant in leading to cohesive action.[28] Indeed, Hakes maintains that party mechanisms operate in a haphazard manner. "The Chief Whip does not link the Government and the backbenchers because his access to the former is too limited." And party caucuses meet infrequently.[29] Hakes argues that after Kenyatta became President he ceased active participation in the day-to-day affairs of Parliament although he retained the prerogatives of Prime Minister. Subsequent leaders of Government business had little impact on cohesion of Parliament.[30] KANU's organization in Parliament, as elsewhere in Kenya, was exceedingly loose.[31] However, if Government was opposed on issues important to it by significant numbers of KANU MPs, President Kenyatta would personally intervene in meetings of the Parliamentary Group of KANU (all KANU MPs).

Part of the very lack of discipline within KANU in Parliament can be attributed to the fact that opposition parties never threatened KANU's majority and thus backbenchers felt free to criticize in speeches and even to vote against Government. The question as to whether or not lack of

[28] For a discussion of patronage as distributed to MPs see Jay E. Hakes, "Patronage and Politics in Kenya: A Study of Backbencher Membership on Statutory Boards," unpublished paper.

[29] *Ibid.*, p. 1.

[30] Jay E. Hakes, "The Parliamentary Party in Kenya," a paper presented at the International Studies Association South-Southwest Regional Meeting, October 15-17, 1970, p. 5.

[31] *Ibid.*, Hakes notes that Whips sometimes voted against the Government.

discipline was a matter of MPs performing representative functions for their constituents remains. If national party organizations were weak, did MPs feel compelled to act in accordance with constituency interests or at least free to do so if they chose? Before trying to answer this question, it is necessary to understand the organizational basis of KANU in Kenya and KANU's relations with categorical groups so that we can begin to come to grips with the pattern of factionalism which has obtained and try to assess its consequences.

The decentralization of KANU has largely been explained as a legacy of a colonial policy which tried to prevent the construction of a united national party which would encompass all ethnic associations in Kenya. Okumu has argued that this important development can be traced back to the 1920s when Local Native Councils were created and that thereafter the colonial regime forced African politics into a district base.[32] The colonial administration proscribed the early nationalist movement, the KAU in 1953, and then banned all other political organizations until June 1955. Subsequently political organization was allowed to proceed on a district base only, so that strong ethnic district organizations appeared by the 1957 Legislative Council elections.[33] Okumu goes further and maintains that the colonial regime successfully fostered "an initial class of individualized administrators, church leaders, and teachers whose behavior was

[32] Okumu, "Charisma and Politics."

[33] *Ibid.*, p. 12. By 1957, a host of ethnically based district associations had appeared among them: The Mombasa African Democratic Union; the Kisii Highlands Abagusii Association of South Nyanza District; the Taita Democratic Union; the Nakuru African Progressive Party.

determined by their desire to please the colonial authority since this was the norm."[34]

Okumu argues that a petty bourgeois class was created in Kenya which had a vested local interest in the district base of Kenya politics. It is not clear, however, why a class commited to colonial authority, perhaps even to the maintenance of colonial styles and values in the post-independence period, and with vested interests in certain land tenure patterns and private economic institutions should also be committed to the district base of political organization. Indeed, Okumu himself points out that elements who opposed the "official class" or Loyalists in Kenya themselves varied from district to district. Thus in Luoland (Nyanza) traditional notables presided over a land-use system they found congenial and opposed the introduction of land consolidation and legal title deeds in freehold which would have fundamentally altered a status system based on land. In Luoland, then, the traditional clan elders opposed the colonial land tenure systems favored by Loyalists, in particular by administrative chiefs and ex-chiefs, who would have benefited and upon whom the colonial regime hoped would be

[34] Okumu has by no means been the only person to call attention to the importance of the district base of politics in Kenya. See also Bennett and Rosberg, *op.cit.,* pp. 33, 41-45; Gertzel, *Politics of Independent Kenya,* pp. 9-10; but Okumu has more than other analysts stressed the normative aspects involved in the creation of "official classes" commitment to the colonial way in Kenya. What is less clear in Okumu's analysis is how inculcation of colonial norms maintained district-based party machines. These seem susceptible of explanation without recourse to analysis based on the absorption of a colonial political culture. Okumu's analysis has also been put forward in an unpublished paper "The Problems of Tribalism in Kenya," and in "The Socio-Political Setting," in Hyden, Jackson, and Okumu, *op.cit.*

founded a middle class of land owners whose property would make them a stable class.[35] In Kikuyuland (Central Province) the opposition to the official classes was led by more highly educated Kikuyus and by urbanized elements in particular, although in both Luoland and Kikuyuland small holders feared that land consolidation would work against them, and the landless in Kikuyuland opposed the Loyalists. Mau Mau recruits could be found among better educated people in urban areas, among trade unionists, and among poor farmers. It was from the latter category that many of the fighters who went to the forests were recruited.[36]

While the policies of the colonial regime certainly weighed heavily on Kenyan politics as it evolved in the 1960s, the colonial inheritance was not the only factor which made for the maintenance of a district base in Kenya politics.

D. Participation, Elections, and Control

Kenya, like many African countries, had a marked increase in political participation in the terminal colonial and immediate independence period. The rise in activity has been treated as mass-type politics. But while the numbers of people voting increased and the number of work stoppages increased, this activity was led by elites: trade union organizers, party officials, better-off farmers were pressing their demands through organizational

[35] Okumu, "Charisma," p. 11. Also see John C. de Wilde, *Experience with Agricultural Development in Tropical Africa*, Vol. II (Baltimore: Johns Hopkins Press, 1967), pp. 121-156, and Malcolm Valentine, "Continuity and Change in Luo Social Organization," unpublished paper, Kampala, 1965.

[36] See Kaggia, *op.cit.*, and Barnett and Njama, *op.cit.*

87

means. We can agree that there has been an independence style of participation centered around electoral activity and a post-independence style centered around individual petitioning for favors through direct dealing with the bureaucracy and other institutions with resources.[37] The critical point, however, is that the people who led the activities of a mass nature were those who would subsequently be well placed to engage in direct bargaining to further their own interests even when mass political participation was limited and at times curtailed. In other words, district politics in Kenya first fed on and was organized around mass activities.[38] Later the district competition continued between persons well placed to compete as elites contended with each other. However, mass politics was reined in.

The increase in numbers of politically ambitious people who entered new political arenas opened up in the decolonization process gave further impetus to the subnational nature of competitive politics. It also provoked a counterreaction as attempts were made to control this participation. As we shall see, one of the major consequences of intense factionalism was the proliferation of controls designed to lessen the costs of factionalism. But these controls did not eliminate competition among elites in trade unions, cooperatives, KANU branches. What they

[37] Ross, *op.cit.*

[38] I am now using the word "district" very loosely. Not only the administrative district party organizations but also the county councils, municipal councils, and KANU branches, sub-branches, can all be considered part of district, as opposed to national, politics. So can struggle within regional assemblies during the *Majimbo* Constitution period of regionalism. Struggle for control of KANU provincial Vice Presidencies has an immediate national aspect. Sometimes the line is blurred when national figures meddle in district factionalism or trade union branch struggles.

did do was to divorce elites from their own constituencies and in a sense give them more freedom to contend with each other in irresponsible ways.

Kenya had a lot of elections between 1960 and 1966. Stren has traced the electoral process for one municipality, Mombasa, in the 1960s. No African had voted in municipal elections before 1960 and fewer than 1,000 were registered to vote in 1957 and 1958 legislative council elections. By 1961 about 25,000 Africans were registered in Mombasa's district and 75,000 by 1963. Moreover, within a space of four months in 1963, Mombasa Africans could vote for Lower House seats in the National Assembly and for the Senate (Kenya then had a bicameral legislature), and for regional assembly seats and for a municipal council.[39] The year 1963 was a high-water mark both in terms of voting turnout and number of public meetings held. In a Mombasa Senate election, in 1965 only 12 percent of those eligible turned out; more than five times that many that had turned out in 1963. KANU officials had a hard time getting permission to call meetings after 1965 and the KPU was refused permission to hold meetings after 1966. During the period of contraction of electoral activity, Government imposed the rule that no independents could stand; party endorsement was required for local and national elections. In Mombasa, as elsewhere, some individuals who were losing out in KANU struggles became KPU in order to be able to contest elections. Above all, in Mombasa, as elsewhere in the country, intense and bitter factional fighting did not cease as mass electoral activity declined. Newspapers were full of assaults that various leaders made on each other—sometimes physical ones.

In Mombasa, a prominent regional leader, Ronald

[39] Stren, *Factional Politics*.

Ngala, aspired successfully to play a national role. Ngala, however, was vulnerable because of the heterogeneous nature of his coastal constituency. Mombasa town has up-country Luos and Kikuyus and strong trade unions, and there are also important Arab and Swahili elements. The indigenous coastal tribes, often referred to as Mijikenda, are themselves anything but cohesive so that conflict persists between Mijikenda groups. The possibilities for fluid alliances have been many.[40] In this situation, national opponents of Ngala made common cause with his local opponents in an attempt to undercut his base. For example, when it looked as if an Ngala-Mboya alliance was being forged, Mboya's opponents opposed Ngala.

Thus the pattern of national-district ties overlay local ethnic, clan, religious, and occupational conflict in Mombasa. Neither the fact that KANU had relatively little to offer in the way of material rewards nor that elections for offices were curtailed ended factionalism, which continued as a struggle over KANU position and within trade unions and ethnic associations.

This pattern was repeated. In Kenya as a whole, electoral participation declined. In the February 1961 election which was the first general election on a common roll basis, over 880,000 voters, or 84 percent of the then eligible electorate cast ballots. In 1963, the turnout of around 85 percent was still high for the general election. In 1965, Senate by-elections were held. It is true that Kenya was now a *de facto* one-party state since the opposition KADU had dissolved. But KANU branches were not able to prevent independent candidates from contesting elections. Indeed, only three out of twelve official candidates won, although all the independents stood as

[40] *Ibid.*

90

KANU independents.[41] Voting turnout fell precipitously. In all constituencies, turnout was higher in 1963, and there had been some contests in 1963 between candidates of the same party too.[42] In the Little General Election of 1966, the average turnout for all constituencies was 33 percent.[43] In a by-election held in Gem, a KPU area of Central Nyanza, in May 1969, again turnout was very low.

Kenya had its first general election since 1963 in December 1969. In this election, there was some attempt to restrict the ability of anyone to stand as a KANU candidate. The election was a primary election in which candidates had to be KANU members for six months, but anyone could vote in the election. Candidates also had to pass a language test in English. The newspapers reported a fairly high failure rate. Some Nairobi city councillors failed, and farmers and businessmen were also reported as failing. Indeed, hundreds were reported to have failed and only a few of these appealed to the Language Appeals Board.[44] Candidates also had to make a "non-re-

[41] Gertzel, *Politics of Independent Kenya*, p. 59.

[42] In Turkana, in the north, turnout was 5 percent in 1965, 50 percent in 1963; in Muran'ga it was 26 percent compared to 75 percent at the earlier time; in Central Nyanza it was 13 percent as against 88 percent. Mueller, *op.cit.*, p. 30.

[43] Nor was turnout related to the closeness of the election. In the two highest turnouts, the victories were overwhelming. But in them both, prominent candidates stood: Odinga and Kaggia, the former winning, the latter losing.

[44] The newspapers reported failures on an *ad hoc* basis. It was reported that all 10 candidates passed at a Kakamega district sitting and 4 out of 6 passed in Busia district while 49 out of 71 passed at Kisumu and 70 out of 93 in the Rift Valley. But in Nairobi 11 out of 24 were reported to have failed. The language tests were taken under the supervision of the provincial administration. *East African Standard*, November 18, 1969.

turnable deposit" of about $115.[45] This rule worked also to narrow the potential pool of candidates. Still, there was no dearth of would-be nominees. Six hundred and sixteen prospective candidates went before the Executive Committee of KANU and the KANU provincial vice presidents who met two weeks before election day to screen candidates. Only five were rejected on the ground that they did not comply with party rules.[46] Candidates also had to sign an oath of loyalty to KANU, which apparently did not trouble anyone.[47] More troublesome for some elected officials was the rule stating that they must resign their offices to stand for election. One prominent ex-KPU member, the Mayor of Mombasa, at first refused to allow that this rule applied to him. He eventually did not resign his mayoralty and did not stand for Parliament. Many city and town councillors did put themselves forward but others must have been deterred, as was the good Mayor of Mombasa.[48] The rule requiring resignation from an elected post was aimed at restricting the number of candidates who would use a base already won to jump

[45] Candidates for local elections must pay a non-refundable fee of around $30.

[46] Hyden and Leys, "Elections and Politics in Single-Party Systems." In the Tanzania general election of 1965, the TANU National Executive Committee imposed candidates in 15 out of 180 cases. See Bienen, *Tanzania*, p. 402. I do not have information on how many prospective nominees were eliminated by TANU central organs in the 1970 election in Tanzania; in March 1969 the TANU Central Committee rejected more than one quarter of the 400 nominees for TANU branch chairman.

[47] In Mombasa the KANU faction in the saddle at the time sponsored 4 of the 19 candidates standing in the town. This sponsorship had no status and was not a typical pattern. It was decried by KANU National Headquarters. See *East African Standard*, December 4, 1969.

[48] Councillors had been MPs in the past.

off to Parliament. Kenyan leaders feared all along that elections would lead to an increase in tension as political elites or would-be-entrants into the political elite competed.[49] Elaborate security measures were taken at election meetings where supporters could be stirred up against each other.

In 1963-64 the response to increased demands for elite entrance into the political system had been to proliferate the posts available for competition—House and Senate seats, regional assemblies, municipalities. Now both the high-level civil servants and the top leaders were unhappy with the large number of politicians they had to take account of. The demands the top elite feared most were not those of the masses for more schools or clinics or even jobs but those of the political elite for more posts.[50] The top leaders felt that an increase in the number of politicians would lead to costs in terms of payrolls and patronage deals. More importantly, it was feared that power would become so fragmented that the society would become ungovernable. Moreover, while political competition increased and the arenas prolifer-

[49] Government could be extremely direct in limiting competition. In one constituency where Mbiyu Koinange was challenged by a rival considered to be very dangerous to him, the competitor of Kenyatta's close adviser was put in preventive detention three weeks before polling day and thus was unable to stand. Leys and Hyden, *op.cit.*, p. 18.

[50] An increase in the numbers of people who contended for power has been discussed for the terminal colonial periods and the first phase of independence in Africa. It is clear that the very fact of elections in the context of weak institutions led to instability. See Crawford Young, *Politics in the Congo* (Princeton: Princeton University Press, 1965); Herbert Weiss, *Political Protest in the Congo* (Princeton: Princeton University Press, 1967); Richard Sklar, *Nigerian Political Parties* (Princeton: Princeton University Press, 1963).

ated—at the same time resources for competition were not highly centralized and thus competition could not be easily controlled—all organizations and associations were "pressed into the role of supplementary structures for the attainment of status, power, and high salaries."[51] Ethnic associations, trade unions, cooperatives all became stepping stones or bases for political competition rather than institutions primarily designed to carry out their stipulated functions. The constitutional changes after 1964 were designed to let leaders restrict elite competition and participation through administrative means. Preventive detention measures, abolition of regional assemblies, ending of independent candidacies, not allowing the KPU to compete—all were measures designed for the same end.

I have suggested, however, that while participation was restricted from below, elite competition was not effectively restricted. In fact, the number of contested seats went from 84 in 1963 to 96 in 1969.[52] In the 1969 election, only about 47 percent of the registered voters, estimated at around 3½ million, actually went to the polls. Hyden and Leys suggest that the low turnout may have been partly due to apathy and deliberate abstention but it was partly explainable by reference to the voting arrangements.[53] It is true that Kenya, with a population not much less than Tanzania's, although more densely settled, had only around 2,000 polling places while Tanzania had more than eight times as many in its 1970 elections in

---

[51] Richard Sandbrook, "Patrons, Clients and Factions," p. 113.

[52] Jay E. Hakes, "The Weakness of Parliamentary Institutions as a Prelude to Military Coups in Africa," paper presented at 43d Annual Meeting of the Southern Political Science Association, Gatlinburg, Tennessee, November 11-13, 1971.

[53] Hyden and Leys, *op.cit.*, p. 17.

which the turnout was 72 percent.[54] In Kenya, there was great unevenness in polling places per district. Mombasa, with an electorate of over 82,000 voters, had 16 polling places for 5 seats. In Kwale district, with 60,500 voters, there were "several" polling stations for two contested seats. In Kilifi district, in which there were more than 10,000 voters and three contested seats, there were 33 polling stations. In Taita/Taveta district, with three seats, there were 17 stations for over 30,000 voters. Lamu district had 22 stations for 10,648 voters and two seats. Tana River had almost twice the voters for the same number of stations as Lamu. Of course, population densities varied.[55]

It is also true that Kenya had voted over two days in 1963 and had only one day's polling in 1969. Many voters were time-barred in Nairobi, Mombasa, and Kakamega. Lines did get unruly at some places as the deadline drew near and riot police intervened.[56] Still, Nairobi's turnout was only around 50 percent. The history of declining turnouts noted above was to be continued in 1970 when a by-election was held because the courts upheld a challenge to one of the December 1969 results. In this by-election, around 25 percent turned out.[57]

[54] *Ibid.* For a discussion of registration laws and ease of access to registration and voting see Stanley Kelley, Richard Ayres, and William Bowen, "Registration and Voting: Putting First Things First," *American Political Science Review* (June 1967), pp. 359-379.

[55] The figures are from the *East African Standard*, December 5, 1969.

[56] KANU's election spokesman, Dr. Mungai, thought it likely that two days' polling would be the rule for the next election. *East African Standard*, December 9, 1969.

[57] There were some 42,900 voters in a by-election in Ndhiwa constituency. In the 1969 General Election, 27 percent had

Turnout was low in the 1969 elections, but well-placed persons flocked to compete. Five lecturers at the university resigned to fight the 1969 election.[58] Three mayors resigned; all subsequently lost. Many city councillors contested too. Education officers, labor union leaders, teachers, chairmen of Government boards and corporations, and civil servants were prominent aspirants.[59] There was an average of nearly four candidates for the 158 seats with as many as 10 candidates in some contests.[60] Urban seats tended to attract large numbers of candidates.[61] Since the urban areas are multitribal, individuals could assume that their opponents would split votes on ethnic grounds.[62] Hyden and Leys state that all their con-

---

turned out. One would expect fall-off in the by-election. Interestingly, the number of polling places had been increased from 11 to 24 from 1969 to 1970. W. O. Oyugi, "The Ndhiwa By-Election," *East Africa Journal*, Vol. 7, No. 10 (October 1970), 4-11.

[58] Their resignation was ruled by the Registrar of University College, Nairobi; it was not directly compelled by Government.

[59] There were complaints in the letters to the editors of the press that highly trained technical personnel like lecturers and doctors were trying to become MPs and as a consequence their scarce skills would be lost to the nation.

[60] Hyden and Leys, *op.cit.*, p. 18. Because there were many candidates, 45 percent of the winners had less than a majority and some had as little as 25 percent. There were no runoffs.

[61] *Ibid.*, p. 19. Nairobi had an average of 5.6 candidates for its 8 seats. In the local government elections which were first held in February 1970 but then postponed, more than 150 people announced that they would contest 10 seats. *East African Standard*, January 23, 1970.

[62] Candidates stood as clan candidates in rural areas. In some cases, the tribal base of rural politics was made clear also. One newspaper report had it that: "the Dumra people of Kwale had decided to return the Assistant Minister in the Office of the Vice

stituency reports emphasized the priority of tribe in urban areas. They note that students who were interviewed shared a commitment to clan and tribe although they pressed for more efficient manipulation by their own representatives of the already existing system.[63]

It had been clear even before the 1969 election that the towns had ceased to provide a forum for nontribal appeals.[64] Indeed, aside from Nairobi where Mboya, a

President, Mr. R. S. Matano, unopposed. . . ." *East African Standard*, November 26, 1969.

[63] Hyden and Leys, *op.cit.*, pp. 19, 26. University students went out and did constituency reports on the 1960 election.

[64] Not only Nairobi and Mombasa, with populations given in the 1969 census as 509,286 and 247,073 respectively, are mixed by race and tribe. The Rift Valley towns, Nakuru and Eldoret, with populations of 47,151 and 18,196 are also very mixed. The heterogeneity of these towns has meant that a challenge to the ethnic political leader who was rurally based might be made via control of a town's KANU organization in the struggle for district control. Some towns like Kisumu with a population of 32,431 or Thika, 18,387, are dominated by one tribal group, in these cases Luo and Kikuyu, respectively. (All population figures are from the *Statistical Abstract*, 1970, Statistics Division of the Ministry of Finance and Economic Planning, Government of Kenya, 1970, p. 15, Table 15.) *The Kenya Population Census*, 1969, also published by the Statistics Division, 1970, breaks down provinces and districts by tribe. But it does not break down towns except for Nairobi. And no tribal breakdown by parliamentary constituency or wards is given for Nairobi. Thus it is not possible to compare census data with the gross votes published in the 1969 returns. One would have to have the election ward figures and to know census data by tribe in the wards to see if there had been any cross-tribal voting. Observers of the voting in Kericho, Nakuru, and Eldoret felt that the voting was highly tribal. In Kericho, one Kikuyu ran against men with Kipsigis, Kisii, and Luhya names and almost beat a Kipsigis candidate. Continued Kikuyu migration into the Rift Valley towns made Kikuyu candidates viable there. Indeed, it was alleged that

Luo, had won in a tribally mixed constituency in 1963 and where early voting patterns had shown some tribal crosscutting, the towns after independence did not provide a context for nontribal politics. The politics of Mombasa was the politics of an array of ethnic and racial coalitions.[65] In Nakuru, tribe was the main distinction.

What had happened in Kenya was that in the years since independence no national party organization had appeared which could slate candidates without reference to tribal affiliation. Leaders wanted to run in their own home areas. Moreover, while in the pre-independence elections of 1957 and 1960 constituencies cut across tribal lines, by 1969 constituencies were tribal with the

some Kikuyu were run against a major Kikuyu candidate to deliberately split the Kikuyu vote.

[65] In 1966, the KPU contested two constituencies, one in Nairobi East and the other in Nakuru. It polled 41 percent of the vote. One analyst (Koff, *op.cit.*, p. 59) saw this heavy KPU urban vote as evidence of relatively strong dissent from Government policies. Another observer (Harbeson, *op.cit.*, p. 2) suggested that the voting in the two urban constituencies may have been governed as much by existing personal and ethnic loyalties as disapproval of the Government's record since independence. There were, however, no voting surveys done which might have established voter attitudes and whether or not the major issues of land policy, nationalization, social services cut across ethnic and personal factional groupings. The continuing influx of Kikuyu into Nakuru and Nairobi cut in different directions since many of those who came in were landless and remained unemployed in the cities. But the newer residents could not have voted in 1966 since the last voter registration had been taken in 1962. Even Kikuyu voters sympathethic to the landless might have voted for KANU rather than the KPU which stressed the need for thorough-going land reform if these Kikuyu thought Government had done a lot in this area or if tribal loyalties prevailed.

exception of the towns. But in the towns, competition for jobs and spoils on a tribal basis had become dominant. It was in the towns in which intense competition took place for licenses and loans for African traders and businessmen who were now replacing Asians. Even in municipal and Civil Service jobs, it was felt that competition was taking place on tribal lines. The towns rather than being melting pots were becoming the major locus of friction because tribal feelings had increasingly been polarized and the towns were the place where people of different tribal origin were in the closest contact with each other. Tribal feeling was often expressed as anti-Kikuyu feeling because it was Kikuyus who were perceived to be controlling Government, new jobs, and loans. And it was Kikuyu who had probably spread over the widest area of settled Kenya and into many towns.[66] But as unemployment continued to be a growing problem in Kenya and arable land became increasingly scarce, by

[66] By 1948, one-third of the Kikuyu population lived outside their home districts of Kiambu, Nyeri, and Muran'ga. There were over 330,000 Kikuyu migrants, and Kikuyu were already the first or second most populous group in 14 of Kenya's 36 districts at that time. Despite the forced repatriation of Kikuyu to their homeland during Mau Mau, by 1962 more than 715,000 Kikuyu were outside their home areas; this was 44 percent of Kenya's Kikuyus. The 1948 census showed that about 42 percent of Kiambu Kikuyu, 32 percent of Nyeri Kikuyu, and 22 percent of Muran'ga Kikuyu lived outside their home district. Soja, *op.cit.*, pp. 54-55.

The second largest group of migrants are Luhya who have moved in a more concentrated way to areas near traditional places of settlement. Luo have migrated outside Kenya to Uganda and Tanzania and have been concentrated in their migration to Nairobi, Mombasa, and to certain areas of occupational specialty in Kenya. *Ibid.*, p. 55.

no means were all tribal tensions Kikuyu vs. non-Kikuyu.[67]

Although factional and tribal competition was fierce in some towns, it was not always closely correlated with higher voter turnout. Nor can we lump together intense competition and large numbers of candidates, since some seats were hotly contested between fewer candidates. But districts with relatively larger numbers of educated and better-off people did have more candidates per seat. Within Central Province, which was the most developed area of the country and which had a high turnout of 66.8 percent, turnout was variable by amount of development per district. Hyden and Leys argue that the higher the level of development, the larger are the economic stakes, the keener the competition, and the more funds spent on electoral organization.[68] But while this seems to work for Central Province it does not work for the towns or for Nyanza which had many would-be MPs but low turnout. Once again, we must make the distinction between elite competition and mass turnout.[69]

It has been important for the development of factionalism and elite competition in Kenya that elections take place and these elections do help make Kenya a repre-

[67] For a stress on Luo-Kikuyu tensions, see Stanley Meisler, "Tribal Politics Harass Kenya," *Foreign Affairs*, Vol. 49, No. 1 (October 1970), pp. 111-121.

[68] Hyden and Leys, *op.cit.*, p. 22. Turnout was well above three-quarters in the more prosperous Kikuyu districts of Nyeri, Kiambu, and Nyandarua but lower than 60 percent in Kirinyaga and closer to 50 percent in Muran'ga, the poorer Kikuyu districts.

[69] Also, we would have to consider all the relevant factors if we tried to assess the relationship between competition and turnout. Ease of access for voting would have to be considered.

sentative system, as I shall argue below, but it is also clear, as we have seen, that Government has imposed strong constraints over the electoral system which have worked to narrow mass participation. The restrictions on participation in party politics from below have worked to emphasize the personalistic aspects of Kenya politics which were already strong since they rested on an ethnic base. There has been little investment in party building at the top and the leaders have made it difficult to build a national party system. KANU remained a congeries of district and subdistrict, personal and ethnic machines. Insofar as a national party system has existed in Kenya politics it is one of patron-client ties built around individuals who cross into each other's districts and/or organizations.

The perception of KANU's weakness as an institution has hindered the possibilities of strengthening it since politicians have not believed that central KANU institutions could carry their careers. Therefore few efforts were made to get beyond some critical point where KANU institutions could be used to strengthen the center and be the vehicle for political power for individuals. The one exception in political careers was that of Tom Mboya whose original base of power was Nairobi where he organized the trade union movement and subsequently founded the Peoples Convention Party which did not have a tribal base.[70] It was Mboya, who as Secretary General of KANU, did try, intermittently, to build a base within KANU for his own power. In part, Mboya did not have a natural Luo base since he was not from the Luo heartland and since Oginga Odinga preempted Luo political loyalties. Toward the end of his life, which was cut

---

[70] I discuss below Kaggia's and Odinga's attempt to create a class-based party outside KANU after failing within it.

short by assassination in 1969, Mboya was trying to build a district base in South Nyanza. But he was one major politician who relied at times heavily on KANU at the center. Mboya was also frustrated by other contenders in Kenya who chipped away at his own trade union base and who had district bases of power which could not easily be attacked from the center because central resources were weak and because ethnic loyalties were strong.

KANU has been made up of district and subdistrict associations which have their own bosses. At times, a dominant figure emerged, like Odinga in Central Nyanza, where his hold on Luo loyalties was very strong. Elsewhere, as on the Coast, a prominent leader like Ronald Ngala did not have a secure ethnic base and his enemies at the center were able to maneuver among his enemies locally. Moreover, the town of Mombasa provided the jobs and posts and trade union organizations for Ngala's opponents to wield against him. Yet a different factional pattern existed among the Kamba where Paul Ngei purported to be a tribal spokesman and was often successful in promoting this role for himself but had to contend with a part of his land being organized against him on clan lines. Sometimes, a subgroup of a tribe supported an important leader, as when Martin Shikuku was "the voice of Butere," an area of Luhya settlement. In all of these cases, leaders saw themselves as bosses of an area and rather explicitly recognized that they were operating local political machines.[71] That is, the main concern of

[71] See George Bennett, "Opposition in Kenya," in *Opposition in the New African States*, University of London, Institute of Commonwealth Studies, No. 4 (October 1967-March 1968), pp. 55-64.

Hyden and Leys described different kinds of machines in the

the bosses' party organizations was to distribute rewards to supporters and to mobilize support for leaders. This support included getting votes in parliamentary elections and local elections, and KANU district and branch elections. It must be emphasized that elections counted in Kenya despite the fact that they were often highly constrained by administrative procedures and despite the fact that neither KADU nor the KPU came close to parliamentary parity with KANU. It makes a difference for political competition and participation whether a one-party system comes into being through electoral majorities and subsequently overwhelming electoral dominance or whether the single party is legislated into existence or uses purely administrative-coercive means to achieve dominance. The KANU Government did make it hard for oppositions to function by sometimes refusing to register a party or by prohibiting meetings or forcing MPs who left KANU to contend new elections in 1966 (with *ex post facto* legislation) or even by physically intimidating oppositionists in certain elections as apparently happened in Kaggia's Kandara election in 1966, and even jailing opposition leaders as was done to Kaggia and later to Odinga. And the carrot as well as the stick was used to

---

1969 elections: (1) The personal clientele of a rich, professional incumbent or a newcomer with political experience. These displayed organizational strength and financial clout. (2) A second type often closely linked with the first was the machine of the party elite. Candidates who were close to Kenyatta invoked him and their ties to him. (3) The long-standing factional machines of individuals outside the President's inner core. These are essentially the organizations of the wealthier and more educated members of particular tribes. Hyden and Leys, *op.cit.*, pp. 26-27. Their machine types are loose descriptions rather than systematic typologies of kinds of machines.

co-opt first KADU and then KPU members by providing jobs or membership on important loan or statutory boards.[72] Still, all this took place within a context where elections occurred and leaders had to mobilize support. National leaders had to be able to hold their constituencies. They had to make a good showing in elections and where possible use their influence to help their supporters win elections. In 1966, Kenyatta himself had to campaign in Kandara constituency against Kaggia, then the Deputy Leader of the KPU, to demonstrate not so much that Kenyatta remained an unchallengeable national leader but that he, Kenyatta, was still the dominant Kikuyu leader who could not be challenged in his own home ethnic base.[73]

That national leaders had to fight elections meant that they had to go to their constituents to renew support. The necessity to mobilize support, however, was not confined to periodic, if relatively frequent, elections. National leaders had to be able to demonstrate to each other and to Kenyatta that their constituencies were solid. This meant dominating in local factional struggles which frequently took place in the arena of KANU branch and district elections.[74] In these arenas, it was necessary to

[72] For the use of the carrot and the stick against KPU people see Mueller, *op.cit.* Hakes, in "Parliamentary Party," also has interesting material on the use of patronage to influence MPs.

[73] Kaggia's opponent won an overwhelming victory in the Kandara election although Kaggia claimed not only that voters were intimidated at the polls but also that the election officials juggled the votes. (Personal interviews and Kaggia's manuscript.)

[74] After 1966, KANU was organized with a Vice President as head of each of Kenya's seven provinces. These were Central Province, made up almost exclusively of Kikuyu areas; Nyanza, which was largely, although not completely, Luo; the Rift Valley, which had increasing numbers of Kikuyu migrants into

line up support of those who would vote in the elections for branch or district chairman or committee members. There were also elections for other officers, e.g., secretaries and treasurers. No matter what the constitutional provisions, elections were held under various arrangements. This is one reason why it was important for leaders to mobilize as much support as they could. It was not always clear, even in an oligarchical setting, just who would count.[75] Moreover, leaders wanted control of district councils or municipal councils, where a chair-

Kalenjin areas where a number of smaller tribes, e.g., Masai, Kipsigis, Nandi, live and where there are also numbers of Luhya and Luo on tea estates, in the towns, and in some rural areas; Eastern Province, with large numbers of Kamba but also Embu and Meru who are related to Kikuyu; Western Province where there are many different tribes with especially significant numbers of Luyha who are themselves broken into many subgroups; Coast Province with Mijikenda people and the inhabitants of Mombasa; the sparsely settled Northern Province; and Nairobi, which has its own Vice President and which is close to half Kikuyu. Below the Provincial level are Kenya's districts. Excluding Nairobi, Kenya has 40 districts. The districts vary widely in population. The three northern districts are all under 100,000 each, while large districts in Nyanza Province are all over 650,-000. These districts are usually fairly ethnically homogenous, at least insofar as tribal groups are concerned. But often, the designation "tribe" includes different subgroups who may be inhabiting the same district. At times, a district will include elements of major tribes. This is true where there are urban centers. Soja, *op.cit.*, p. 54, gives figures for the two largest ethnic groups as a percentage of total size in districts.

[75] Lamb, *op.cit.*, confirms this point. He notes that in Muran'ga district it was hard to count the opposition or to mobilize support. The locational KANU organizations were fragmented, and factions did not possess good enough information to predict with accuracy support that they were likely to get. Since annual delegates' conferences were not being held, nor were party conferences, anyone could claim chairmanships.

manship could provide the base for opposition to a KANU district or branch leader. The constituencies might overlap but not be precisely the same. Leaders had to demonstrate strength in a number of arenas, including trade union organizations, if they operated in an area of rural workers or in urban settings. Leaders wanted to be perceived as the spokesmen for ethnic groups. This meant that they had to try to accumulate power first in the ethnic/district setting. But the many arenas and the relatively few resources of most leaders have meant that it is difficult to do this, and many national leaders have been vulnerable in their home areas. Other national leaders infringe on their territories.

Aside from Kenyatta himself, the one Kenyan national leader who has seemed most secure in his own home base has been Oginga Odinga in Central Nyanza (his authority in South Nyanza was for a time challenged by Tom Mboya). Yet it was Odinga's very support in Luoland which cast him, often despite his own claims and desires, as a Luo leader. Odinga was able to centralize his authority over time in Luoland; he was able both to consolidate power around a traditional base and to become *the* spokesman for Luo. But he was not able to maintain a national position in the face of Kenyatta's opposition. That is, having a strong local base did not guarantee Odinga a national position although it made him a national figure who had to be taken account of and contended with.

Elsewhere, ethnic leaders were less successful in consolidating their base either because their province or sometimes even district was less homogenous—e.g., Ronald Ngala on the Coast—or because there have been other major ethnic leaders—i.e., the Kikuyu leaders below Kenyatta—or where the ethnic group is so fragmented that no one leader can emerge for long—i.e., among the Luhya. Kenyatta's historical position has been unique in that he was able to become the spokesman for and then personification of Kikuyu nationalism at a time when Kikuyu nationalism and Kenyan nationalism were joined for at least many years during the anti-colonial struggle.[76] Subsequently, Kenyatta, as Head of State, was transformed into the Father of the Country, Mzee the Elder. But he too became, for Luo at least, a tribal leader of Kikuyu after Mboya's assassination and the extreme heightening of Luo-Kikuyu tensions.

National leaders then have periodically been forced back to their ethnic base. This happened to Odinga and Kaggia who made pan-tribal and class claims on Kenyans. It happened to Mboya who tried to build an ethnic base where he never had one in Luoland. And it even happened to Kenyatta with his vast prestige in Kenya, in Africa, and abroad.

It has been argued elsewhere that the very process of contending in elections accentuates the importance of ethnicity in Africa since parties often have an ethnic base and opinion leaders emphasize ethnic identification as a primary criterion for choosing a party. The dependence of village voters on ethnic labels to determine which party to support heightens their own sense of ethnicity.[77]

---

[76] These nationalisms were never completely harmonious; many non-Kikuyu viewed Mau Mau with suspicion. See Rosberg and Nottingham, *op.cit.*, for a discussion of Kikuyu nationalism.

[77] Observers of Nigerian politics have frequently linked elections to a rise in ethnic conflict. See Paul Anber, "Nigeria and the Ibos," *Journal of Modern African Studies*, Vol. 5, No. 2 (September 1967), pp. 163-180 and James O'Connell, "The Inevitability of Instability," in *ibid.*, 181-192. Also see Young, *op.cit.*, and Weiss, *op.cit.* for analyses of elections and ethnicity in the Congo.

In Kenya, too, the fact that there were many elections meant that factions were often tied to ethnic groups for purposes of organizing votes. These ethnic groups were sometimes clans in the rural areas or ethnic associations in the towns. In Mombasa, race and religion provided loyalties to organize around.

Tribe has not usually been the major unit in the factional pattern of Kenya politics. Kenyans refer to tribes like Kikuyu or Luo or Masai. But while individuals may identify themselves as part of one of these groups and may see others as belonging to other tribes, factional groups are usually subtribal. Factional alliances also can cut across tribes when high level political leaders create their coalitions in order to compete at the center. They put together a group which may contain individuals from different tribes and subtribes. Certain groups which are described as tribes have great difficulty in acting as a solidary group at any time. This is true for the Luhya, a large tribe as listed in the census, but a group without cohesion and with many local splits and internal distinctions.

In a politics of factional alliances as fluid as Kenya's, subgroups move in and out of dominant alliances. Tribal solidarity can be invoked against others when the tribe is internally divided. This happens among Kikuyu. Mboya and Odinga tried to center Luo allegiances around themselves and each had his own political machine. After Mboya's assassination, great emphasis was placed on Luo unity among Luo. At the same time, oathing took place among Kikuyu in order to bind Kikuyu together. In times of crises, leaders try to create tribal unity. But the more common pattern is that of fragmented ethnic groups which are called tribes but in which subgroups compete with one another and can often be detached from the main group and brought into a new factional grouping. Individual leaders claim to speak for subgroups and to "bring them into" a factional alliance through their attachment to some national network.

E. FACTIONALISM AND REGIME SUPPORT

The Kenya setting is one in which the politics of patron-client networks cuts across both occupational and ethnic groups. The type of political participation that attaches to the patron-client and machine modes of politics is one in which interests of various forms and types associate, conflict, and change alliances and in which Government responds to relatively strong interest groups on an *ad hoc* basis. The rhetoric of plebiscitary decision making in which "the people" are publicly said to be at center stage cannot obscure this reality in Kenya any more than Leninist forms of party organization should necessarily be taken seriously elsewhere in Africa. It would be less accurate to conceive of party in Kenya as a linking mechanism between center and periphery or even as filling the gap between the parochial and national spheres than to see it simply as an institution which provides numerous arenas for political competition and also which in given places and times transmits demands upward and sometimes provides support for Government.

Kenyatta's own leadership style can be viewed in the Kenya context as an adaptation to the realities of a non-egalitarian society yet one which is still basically not stratified by class. This is the leadership style of the patron or "big man" or what in Kenya is called the *samaki kubwa* or "big fish." Hyden and Leys point to the character of the political culture of the East African peasantries and specifically to the tradition of the "big

man" who can provide patronage and protection for local clientele, "a tradition which accepts inequality as natural and sees politics as a means of solving individual and local problems through the provision of grass-roots support for the 'right' patron."[78]
We must take a certain care with political culture arguments. For one thing, not all Kenya's ethnic communities exhibit the same pattern of authority relationships. For another, Hyden and Leys themselves point out that the "big men" who emerge from acquiring wealth in the local communities in Kenya are not generally distrusted. Wealth can be taken as a sign of fitness to lead.[79] Critics of Kenya are fond of pointing out that those who are not dressed in tie and coat or who do not speak English feel ill at ease in dealing with educated people. The notion here is that the "big fish" has cut himself off from the local community. Yet two different samples responded to the contrary. Nyeri (Kikuyu) farmers were asked:

> "If you and some of your friends went to (mention leader) with a suggestion, would he listen to you or just ignore what you said?" They were in turn asked about the chief, the District Commissioner, or District Officer, the MP, the local KANU leader. In no case did the expectations of a favorable reception drop below 90 percent.[80]

A sample of Kenya secondary students was asked to agree or disagree with the statement: "Ordinary people should feel free to give advice to our political leaders or to ask them for help." Eighty-seven percent of the Kenya

[78] Hyden and Leys, *op.cit.*
[79] *Ibid.*, p. 25.
[80] Ronald Stockton, "Aspects of Leadership in Nyeri," IDS Staff Paper No. 107, Nairobi, n.d. Stockton sampled 349 landowners chosen randomly from a district registry.

Party Politics

sample agreed, compared to 80 percent of a Tanzania sample of secondary students.[81]

No one to my knowledge has described local politics in Kenya the way that one observer has described local politics in Kita, a Mali town where extensive political participation by all segments of the community was one of the cornerstones of the political system.[82] However, some of the characteristics of a participant system do apply in Kenya. Retention of individuals in major political roles reflects their success in obtaining more support from the public than their rivals are able to get.[83] True, some of the inner core around Kenyatta have no clear political base of their own and some have been propped up with administrative support, but by and large political leaders must demonstrate their local base of strength. While Kenya does not share with Kita the characteristic that

[81] David Koff and George Von Der Muhll, "Political Socialization in Kenya and Tanzania," in Kenneth Prewitt, ed. *Education and Political Values: An East African Case Study* (Nairobi: East African Publishing House, 1971), p. 92. The authors selected a subsample of secondary students' responses drawn from Kenya and Tanzania. The samples were selected from a much larger sample. They comprised 20 pupils drawn at random from each of six secondary schools with two of the secondary schools being represented by forms II, IV, and VI. They sought to include both boarding and day schools, coeducational and unisex schools, schools representing both government and religious sponsorship, and schools with different locations. The subsample did not constitute a statistically representative microcosm of East African students although it did include a full range of school environments. About 70 percent of the students in Tanzania and 80 percent of those in Kenya were boys. See "Appendix A—Scope and Nature of the Survey," in *ibid.*, pp. 101-102.

[82] Nicholas S. Hopkins, *Popular Government in an African Town* (Chicago: University of Chicago Press, 1972).

[83] *Ibid.*, p. 218.

111

political pressure from the bottom is far more important than Government initiative from the center, people and institutions in Kenya are responsive to popular pressure. A regime can be responsive to popular pressure by being representative even though there is no norm that all people will participate in the making of decisions that affect them. That is, the regime can deliver goods and services which are highly valued and it can provide for turnover in the individuals who represent without actually altering the relationship between elites and non-elites. Kenya's factional system does both these things.

It would be a mistake to dismiss the many elections Kenya has had because participation has narrowed and the elections have not been completely open and unrestricted by Government. Elections have been important although they led to a renewal of the *kind* of elite that remained in power. Turnover of individuals gives people the feeling that there is a response possible to poor, that is ineffectual, representation.[84]

Elections have served as the battleground for intra-elite competition and as the connecting link between elite and mass. Indeed, one of the consequences of a system of controlled elections was to provide for some representation by elites of mass demands and to provide channels for political participation without altering the basic relations of elites and masses. Hyden and Leys put it with reference to the 1969 election:

[84] The 1969 general election resulted in 93 new faces in a Parliament of 158 elected constituencies. Among the casualties were 5 Ministers and 13 Assistant Ministers. Half of the former MPs who actually contested seats lost. There was an infusion of trade union leaders into the new Parliament but it is not at all clear that this represented any alteration of the political elite since trade unionists had used their organizations to move into the regime before.

. . . the voter was being offered participation in the choice of a government; and consequently this reinforced his conviction, based on tradition and experience, that the significance of the election was to choose a local patron who would do most for his particular constituents within the framework permitted by the government.[85]

They, however, apply this same analysis to Tanzania's elections. They attribute the limited role of elections and the renewal of a kind of elite to the structure of the electoral system which ensured it and which I have outlined above. But while Kenyan and Tanzanian elections may be subject to a similar analysis, Kenya has had a much more personalistic politics, more open factionalism, and much more importance has been given to tribal distinctions.[86] Here it is the open factional nature of Kenya's politics that I want to stress.

[85] Hyden and Leys, *op.cit.*

[86] Tanzania has more salient religious distinctions than Kenya. But interestingly, in the light of all the attention given to tribal tensions in Kenya, one observer found the following.

Question	Answers	No. Replying	%
Which group is more important for you?	1. Tribal	36	7
	2. Professional, occupational	97	20
	3. Religious	117	24
	4. Community service	33	7
	5. Social (club, recreational)	9	2
	6. Blank	192	40
		484	

The question was asked of a sample compiled from urban and peri-urban residents in Mombasa and Nairobi. Hopkins, "Code Book," p. 8. Professor Hopkins is not responsible for any of my use of the material he kindly made available.

Koff and Von Der Muhll, *op.cit.*, p. 94 found an intensity of preference for religion rather than tribe when they asked primary and secondary students: "Which is more important to you, your tribe or your religion?"

113

We are familiar with the literature on machines which has stressed that they are organizations which rely characteristically upon the attraction of material rewards rather than enthusiasm for political principles. A great deal flows from this understanding of a particular type of political organization. The party machine's central function is not to frame or to discipline its members in the framing of the policies of government. Elections are important but this is so because they are elections for jobs, and winning them gives access to more jobs; internal division over policy questions is supposed to play little part in elections. To say that a party is not policy-oriented does not mean that policy issues never arise, but rather that cleavages within the party are not over policy issues. In analyses that stress material rewards as a goal of a political organization and its members, patronage and corruption are also emphasized.[87]

In Kenya, cleavages inside KANU have rarely been over policy issues with the exception of the split which led eventually to the KPU formation where land issues and socioeconomic issues in general were articulated. The muting of issues has been one consequence of factionalism in Kenya. The unwillingness of the regime to let competitive party politics flourish as viable opposition politics hinders the development of issue politics, too. We have also noted the penetration of all institutions with factional politics and thus the politicization of functional and associational groups that then had to be controlled with the same *raison d'être* which had operated to limit party politics. As KANU itself often ceased to be the significant arena for factional encounters, the press became full of reports of trade union conflict at the cen-

[87] From Bienen, "One-Party Systems in Africa," p. 113.

ter, and in rural areas, school committees and cooperatives often became the forum for factional struggle.[88]
This has serious consequences for the ability of institutions to carry out their stipulated functions.[89] But it does
not mean that Kenya's regime is moribund or that Kenya
is a praetorian society.[90]

Huntington's characterization of a praetorian society
is one in which there is a general politicization of social
forces and institutions. "Countries which have political
armies also have political clergies, political universities,
political bureaucracies. . . ."[91] These institutions involve
themselves in politics not just over issues which concern

[88] Lamb, *op.cit.*, p. 15, suggests that in one district even when
factional encounters fell off in KANU after 1966, party standing
was still an important qualification for competition elsewhere.

[89] Frank Holmquist and Jack Parsons have described the
impact of increased political activity on a traders' association in
South Nyanza between 1961 and 1963. The association was
neglected as an economic enterprise as factional politics were
fought out within it. It eventually became abandoned by leaders
who found other political vehicles. See their "Interest Groups and
Political Change: Traders' Associations in Kisii District, Kenya
and Kampala, Uganda," University of East Africa Social Science
Conference, Dar-es-Salaam, December 27-31, 1970.

[90] The idea of praetorian societies has made an impact on
recent studies of militaries in developing countries in part because its proponents have often been critical of the idea that
the military is best suited to modernize developing countries.
Also, their analyses have moved away from a discussion of organizational qualities of armed forces and focused instead on
society at large and more specifically on patterns of political
participation and institutionalization. See Samuel P. Huntington,
Political Order in Changing Societies (New Haven: Yale University Press, 1966). Amos Perlmutter, "The Arab Military
Elite," *World Politics*, Vol. 22, No. 2 (January 1970), pp. 269-
300.

[91] Huntington, *op.cit.*, p. 194.

them but over issues which affect society as a whole. The praetorian society, in Huntington's analysis, does not have specialized political institutions which mediate conflict. It does not have agreed-on rules of the game for resolving conflict.[92] Another important feature of a praetorian society in Huntington's description is the fragmented nature of political power. "It [power] comes in many forms and in small quantities. Authority over the system as a whole is transitory. . . ."[93] Huntington distinguishes between types of praetorian society. The types are characterized by levels of participation. Societies with weak political institutionalization can be oligarchical praetorian, radical praetorian, and mass praetorian, depending on how broad the level of participation is. Conflict becomes more intense as participation increases.

In a praetorian oligarchy politics is a struggle among personal and family cliques; in a radical praetorian society the struggle among institutional and occupational groups supplements that among cliques; in mass praetorianism, social classes and social movements dominate the scene.[94]

Huntington does not deal with Tropical African cases in much detail, but he does classify the African pattern as one of radical praetorianism.

[92] *Ibid.*, p. 196.

[93] *Ibid.*, pp. 196-197. Huntington has much more to say about praetorian societies in Latin America, the Middle East, and Asia than in Africa. He compares Africa in the 1960s to Latin America in the 1820s and finds a decay of political authority and institutions in both. Since Africa was less stratified than Latin America and since the middle class broke into politics at a later historical period, radical rather than oligarchical praetorianism is said to have been produced (p. 209).

[94] *Ibid.*, pp. 197-198.

116

If we were to put a label on Kenya—using these types based on clusters of characteristics having to do with participation and institutionalization, the clique, machine, faction—personalistic aspects of Kenya would seem to require the label of oligarchical praetorian type.[95] On the other hand it could be argued that Kenya has more participation than many other African countries if we consider direct group-to-group relationships and the local participation that exists in many rural communities.[96] Nongovernmental institutions have become politicized and faction-ridden, and power is fragmented in Kenya, as elsewhere in Africa. And while in Kenya both Civil Service and military have been strongly institutionalized as compared to other African countries, they are unable nonetheless to exert authority over the whole territorial entity they rule.[97] That is, a great deal of political life

[95] Huntington's analysis does not appear to be an ideal type. Real societies in time and place are put into a particular category. Indeed, the discussion proceeds without reference to "pure forms" or caveats about classifying real systems in terms of typological constructs.

[96] When all is said and done it would be extremely difficult to arrive at a meaningful index which would give us measurements for levels and intensity of participation just as it would be hard to measure for institutionalization in terms of adaptability, flexibility, autonomy, and even durability of institutions.

[97] I have discussed the Civil Service above. For a treatment of the Kenya military see Henry Bienen, "Military and Society in East Africa: Thinking Again About Praetorianism," unpublished paper. Kenya has not been without its own tribal competition for positions in the army and police. In 1971, some purges of Kamba officers took place. Kenya has had a relatively well-trained army which maintains close ties to British military services. And the Kenyan army's success in putting down a Somali secessionist movement in the northern part of the country helped work to keep

117

still goes on outside the reach of central rulers. Nor can a ruling personal clique extend its client system in such a way that power flows from the top to all the nooks and crannies. But despite the rhetoric of need for social mobilization and economic development, there is no evidence that Kenya's rulers think they can wield total power. They have limited goals, and the institutions and resources at their disposal are often sufficient unto their ends.

The fact that power is limited tells us a lot, but by no means everything, about the nature of power and authority in a system. While the reach of central institutions may be limited, there still can be authority in a faction-ridden system. There can be agreed-on rules of the game and even stability and support within the system and for its maintenance.

Although Kenya, along with its neighboring East African countries, had an army mutiny in 1964, there has been stability of central authority in Kenya since independence.[98] I say this despite the factionalism, the fact that the Constitution was amended twelve times in a six-year period, the large turnover in Parliament, the assassination of Mboya, and the extreme tribal tension in its aftermath. Kenya has had stable "Cabinet" Government. Patterns of politics did not much alter. Services continued to be provided. Opposition came and went and parties were formed and went out of existence. The

---

rather narrowly defined professional norms viable as action within the scope of the norms was perceived to be feasible.

[98] The Kenya mutiny was more limited in scope and duration as compared to Uganda's and Tanzania's. See Henry Bienen, "Public Order and the Military in Africa: Mutinies in Kenya, Uganda, and Tanganyika," in Bienen, ed., *The Military Intervenes*, pp. 35-70.

regime survived both in terms of personnel and in terms of the way Kenya was governed.

We started this study by noting that criticism of Kenya has been made by many observers to the effect that Kenya is a system run for the benefit of an elite of power and increasingly of wealth and one which is at dead end. These claims have not yet been established. What is clear, however, is that a spoils system, manipulated by party machines, exists underneath and even alongside a leadership at least rhetorically committed to social change and constantly making normative appeals to the party and to society as a whole.[99] What are the consequences? Has the population become cynical and/or apathetic?

I have already noted the tremendous demands that continue to be made in Kenya from below and the enormous energies that continue to be channeled into self-help activities. Still, it is also true that active membership in KANU declined in many parts of the country after independence and that many people of talent and energy went elsewhere to pursue their interests. But this was as much or more a function of opportunities opening up in commercial and agricultural spheres as it was unhappiness with KANU. Kenya is by no means unique in having upwardly mobile individuals use party institutions to achieve economic advantages and then devote full time to pursuing those advantages to the utmost.[100] Thus it is hard to know how many turned away from KANU out of discontent with it or because the pattern of party politics

[99] See Bienen, "Political Parties and Political Machines," in Loficie, p. 205.

[100] Ruthenberg, *op.cit.*, p. 108, interviewed farmers who had turned away from politics or whose interest had lessened as they pursued economic goals.

119

had shifted after independence allowing individuals with different resources to compete more successfully at different times or because they were in it originally for their economic advantages. The absence of operative organizational or constitutional norms to control conflict meant that many losers probably did turn away from party politics. At local levels, there was often no appeal within KANU itself to "due process."[101] The lines of cleavage between "ins" and "outs" hardened.[102] But at middle and upper levels new alliances could be forged and the factional system was so fluid that losers could try to come back in and often succeeded in doing so.[103]

Since the mutiny of 1964, which was undertaken not by officers but by disgruntled enlisted men, the only attempt which has come to light to overturn the system outside the rules of the game was one which implicated thirteen persons. While there were some prominent persons involved including an MP, a Nairobi city councillor, a manager of a Government statutory board, a former KPU youth leader, the plot seemed incredibly poorly conceived and organized.[104] Intra-elite competition has not

---

[101] Lamb, *op.cit.*, describes this in Muran'ga.

[102] Stren, *Factional Politics*, p. 47. The legislation which made party endorsement necessary to stand for office accentuated divisions within KANU.

[103] KPU leaders, and before them KADU leaders, were able to come back in. Trade union leaders have won and lost and won again in complex alignments. See Sandbrook, *op.cit.* Losers can fall very far and very fast in this system too.

[104] Njonjo, *op.cit.* Insinuations were raised during the trials against much more important national figures—the Chief Justice and the Chief of Staff who were both Kamba as was the implicated MP. Njonjo believes that the Kenyatta Government faced severe pressure from the army in 1969 when oathings among Kikuyu were going on. He cites Colin Legum and John Drysdale, *Africa Contemporary Record; Annual Survey and Documents, 1969-*

led to serious threats to the Government from within or from elites who are "out" at a given point.

Factionalism and competition for positions and spoils among elites and restrictions on mass participation since 1963 have not destroyed support from below either. In Hopkins' survey the sample was asked the following questions (Table I).[105]

70 (Exeter: Africa Research Limited), p. B123. It is highly questionable whether army pressure amounted to a "close shave," as Njonjo maintains. It is true that Kenyatta invoked the old freedom fighters in the forests at a rally in April 1971. This could have been taken as a threat to confront the army with force if need be. It also could be taken as a Kikuyu threat against Kamba or anyone else.

[105] Von Der Muhll and Koff, *op.cit.*, p. 74, asked Kenyan and Tanzanian primary and secondary school students whether members of different groups could be trusted. Their results are shown below.

Percentage of Students Who Say that Members of Different Groups Can Be Trusted "Always" or "Usually"

Groups	KENYA SCHOOLS		TANZANIA SCHOOLS	
	Pri-mary	Second-ary	Pri-mary	Second-ary
Fathers	78	92	85	87
Teachers	80	79	86	77
Religious leaders	74	82	90	84
Government leaders	72	57	89	63

David Court and Kenneth Prewitt, in "Nation Versus Region: Social Learning in Kenyan Secondary Schools," IDS Paper, Nairobi, September 1972, gave a rank ordering on basis of proportion of trust in Government expressed by secondary students by province: Coast 1; Central 2; Eastern 3; Rift Valley 4; Western 5; Nyanza 6. The students saw Government doing many things for their family by rank order on basis of proportion: Central 1; Rift Valley 2; Coast 3; Eastern 4; Western 5; Nyanza 6.

121

TABLE I

SATISFACTION WITH GOVERNMENT

How satisfied are you with the general performance of government now in providing for the needs
of the people?

Percent	No.	
9	42	1. Fully dissatisfied
10	50	2. Partly dissatisfied
36	173	3. Partly satisfied
38	183	4. Fully satisfied
7	36	Blank
	484	

In general, how satisfied are you with those who
are now in high positions of government?

Percent	No.	
8	37	1. Fully dissatisfied
13	61	2. Partly dissatisfied
34	164	3. Partly satisfied
36	176	4. Fully satisfied
10	46	Blank
	484	

Now I want to read to you some statements about
the government. Would you indicate what you
believe is true? Do you think that people in the
government:

Percent	No.	
16	78	1. Waste a lot of money paid in taxes?
29	138	2. Waste some of it
44	215	3. Don't waste very much of it
11	53	Blank
	484	

TABLE I—*Continued*

How much of the time do you trust the government to do what is right?

Percent	*No.*	
2	8	1. Never
8	38	2. Seldom
35	169	3. Some of the time
50	240	4. Most of the time
6	29	Blank
	484	

Would you say the government is run for the benefit of all the people, or that it is run by a few big interests (or people) looking out for themselves?

Percent	*No.*	
24	115	1. Few big interests
69	336	2. All the people
7	33	Blank
	484	

How about you personally, do you think that the things the government does are in your interest, or good for you personally?

Percent	*No.*	
19	93	1. No
26	127	2. Don't know
50	244	3. Yes
4	20	Blank
	484	

TABLE I—*Continued*

Some people think of the government as distant, not caring about the average person, while others feel the government listens to people and responds to their needs. How about you, do you feel the government is distant or close?

Percent	No.	
20	95	1. Distant—does not respond
28	135	2. Mixed response—neither
48	229	3. Does listen and respond
4	19	Blank
	478	

SOURCE: Raymond Hopkins, *Code Book, op.cit.*

Since independence, 67 percent of Hopkins' sample see some improvement in their lives, but 84 percent see an improvement in most people's lives (Table II).

TABLE II

PERCEPTIONS OF IMPROVEMENTS

How do you think things have changed since independence? In your own life, for instance, would you say your opportunities and living conditions are:

Percent	No.	
35	168	1. Much improved
30	147	2. Improved a little
21	104	3. The same
11	54	4. Worse
2	11	Blank
	484	

TABLE II—*Continued*

What about for most people in the country? Have
conditions:

Percent	No.	
42	204	1. Much improved
37	180	2. Improved a little
10	48	3. Remained the same
5	25	4. Become worse
6	27	Blank
	484	

SOURCE: Hopkins, *op.cit.*

Ross asked his Nairobi sample about their perceptions
of improvement (Table III).

TABLE III

Perception of Degree of Improvement in Living
Conditions in the City and Personal Living Conditions Since Independence

	Living Conditions in the City (percent)	Personal Living Conditions (percent)
Improved	67	52
Remained the same or don't know	25	36
Grown worse	8	12
	100	100
Sample size	498	498

SOURCE: Marc Howard Ross, "Grass Roots in the
City," p. 264.

And, when people in Hopkins' sample were asked who they thought would be interested in helping a person, they more often named politicians than civil servants. They thought the latter could *deliver* benefits.

TABLE IV

Which do you think would be more interested in helping the person, the political leader or the civil servant?

Percent	No.	
19	93	1. Civil servant
48	234	2. Politician
18	86	3. Both, no difference, do not know
15	71	Blank
	484	

SOURCE: Hopkins, *op.cit.*

TABLE V

If a person wants some help, do you think a civil servant or a political leader would be better able to help you?

Percent	No.	
37	180	1. Civil servant
28	136	2. Politician
20	95	3. Both, cannot tell, do not know
15	73	Blank
	484	

SOURCE: Hopkins, *op.cit.*

126

On the basis of Hopkins' and Ross's data then, it does not appear that Kenyans in two major cities and their environs have become negative about their Government and politicians because of factionalism and the politics of spoils. Data supporting this conclusion have been presented by Ronald Stockton in a study based on interviews with a random sample of 349 farmers in Nyeri district.[106] (Nyeri is a Kikuyu district.) This study states that Nyeri farmers have become intensely aware of economic and social modernization for the rural area. "There is a general feeling that leaders listen to the people and that the people obey them. People feel very efficacious at having African leaders. These they feel understand local problems and are sympathetic to popular feelings, though there is some feeling that bribes and nepotism cancel out many of the benefits of popular rule. They definitely feel that elections make leaders more responsive."[107] (None of the incumbent Nyeri MPs won in the 1969 election.) Stockton goes on to say that leaders are generally thought of as competent, effective, receptive to public opinion, and legitimate.

While there was a considerable element of cynicism regarding the behavior of professional politicians as a class, Stockton calls this "efficacious cynicism." He says peasant farmers distinguish between myth and reality of electoral promises and are offended by unrealistic promises and as the 1969 election showed, willing to replace incumbents. At the same time, MPs are thought to represent the people.

When Stockton asked about Government's performance and policies, his respondents, who were both local

---

[106] Stockton, *op.cit.*   [107] *Ibid.*, p. 5.

leaders who constituted a propertied class, and nonleaders, showed high levels of dissatisfaction.

TABLE VI

ATTITUDES TOWARD MEMBERS OF PARLIAMENT IN NYERI

Questions	"Yes" responses (percent)
Do MPs represent the people (as opposed to some unspecified "other interests")?	71
Can politicians be trusted to keep the promises they make during an election?	15

SOURCE: Ronald Stockton, "Aspects of Leadership in Nyeri," IDS Staff Paper No. 107 (Nairobi, n.d.), p. 6.

TABLE VII

SATISFACTION WITH GOVERNMENT IN NYERI

Is the government doing all it can for this area (Nyeri)? (*percent*)

Response	Leaders	Random Landowners
Yes	54.6	53.0
No	40.0	36.4

The fruits of independence have gone to the rich (*percent*)

Response	Leaders	Random Landowners
agree	74.5	81.9
disagree	23.7	12.0

SOURCE: Stockton, *op.cit.*

Yet when both groups were asked about specific social services, the level of satisfaction rose to the range of 60-70 percent. Stockton, taking into account the high levels of productive self-help in the district concluded that discontent was not necessarily an indication of Government neglect but perhaps more a reflection of social change.[108] I would go further than Stockton to argue that for all the problems of Kenya's economy, the uneven growth and high rate of unemployment, and that for all the difficulties inherent in ethnic tensions, "there is no doubt that living standards rose rapidly in Kenya during the first plan period (1964-69) nor that they were widely distributed."[109] In this time, per capita *monetary* personal consumption grew at an annual rate of 4.3 percent per annum in constant 1964 prices.

For all the talk about Tanzania's emphasis on rural development and Kenya's parasitical urban elite, the Kenya Second Five Year Plan states that 20.6 percent of central Government expenditure over the next plan period will be allocated to agriculture as compared to Tanzania's 20.8 percent.[110] While income gaps between rural and urban areas widened in Kenya, they widened comparatively more in Tanzania in the same period. The

[108] *Ibid.*, pp. 7-8. In a personal communication, Mr. Stockton warns that his data on questions of general efficacy must be taken with care because of translation problems. He notes that his result on the question of "Is Government doing all it can . . ." is perhaps overly anti-system. He states that his findings showed that there was a great deal of "system support" of a diffuse nature but significant disagreement over specifics. There was also a high level of expectations and many demands were made upon the Government distributive mechanisms and this resulted in a high level of "discontent." Support for local leadership was high.

[109] Frank Mitchell, "Macro Aspects of the Plan," *East Africa Journal*, Vol. 7, No. 3 (March 1970), p. 25.

[110] *Ibid.*, p. 24.

gross comparisons between Tanzania and Kenya do not tell us whether it is big or medium or small farmers who are getting particular shares of rural income. If large farmers, especially the remaining European farmers, were getting the benefits of increased agricultural expenditures in Kenya we would not expect rural support for the regime to be widely based.

I examine below the nature of Government tradeoffs in the rural areas. It is not only the benefits to various economic strata that must concern us. Distribution of benefits leads us back to ethnic politics because the politics of distribution in Kenya is perceived by the actors first and foremost in ethnic terms.

IV

Ethnicity and Class

A. ETHNICITY

Communal solidarities have not been breached as yet in Kenya. Indeed, economic development and social change seem to have given greater salience to ethnic considerations through migration patterns and the unevenness of change.[1] The income and educational disparities that we noted at the outset of this study obviously work to accentuate ethnic divisions. Intertribal conflict can be economically based rather than rest on "traditional" animosities. Nonetheless, conflict in society can be perceived as being ethnic rather than occupational or class. Sklar argues that tribalism in new states should be treated as a dependent variable and not as a primordial political force.[2] I also do not like the term primordial because it implies that ethnic identities are "givens," fixed categories, whereas these categories can be created out of a modernizing process and ethnic perceptions can be fed by politicians. Or, politicians can use organizations and wield ideologies to try to change perceptions. Nonetheless, all

[1] See Soja, *op.cit.* and Rothchild, *Ethnic Inequalities in Kenya.* For a study of modernization and ethnic tensions in another African country see Robert Melson and Howard Wolpe, eds., *Nigeria: Modernization and the Politics of Communalism* (East Lansing: Michigan State University Press, 1971).

[2] Richard Sklar, "Political Science and National Integration," *Journal of Modern African Studies,* Vol. 5, No. 1 (May 1967), pp. 1-12.

the assertions in the world that those who compete and conflict on the basis of tribe or race are demonstrating false consciousness do not change the reality that ethnic perceptions are political factors. Moreover, we have to at least take into account that people may put race and tribe above economic interests. That is, they may care more about preserving relative status or control positions than getting more goods and services. Therefore, even if all groups in a society could be shown that certain policies would improve everyone's lot (which is rarely the case) some groups might prefer not to improve their own situations if it meant the improvement of other peoples'. In Africa, politics is often the politics of defense against encroachments by others.[3] Relatively privileged groups may fear that improvements in conditions for relatively low-status groups will allow those groups more success-fully to compete and threaten privileged groups at a later time.

While Kenya does not have any tribal unit within it which is as centralized as the Baganda have been within Uganda, it does have a great deal of tribal self-conscious-ness. Some of this tribal self-awareness has been "tradi-tional"—that is, it predates the colonial impact and is expressed in tribal struggle over land, raiding, etc. But what was critical for Kenya was that economic, educa-tional, social development had been uneven, and that the Kikuyu who were advanced on the indices of develop-ment were also politically cut off during the 1950s. It was the Kikuyu who had led the anti-colonial struggle but who also had come into contact with other tribal

[3] For a discussion along these lines see Martin Kilson, *Political Change in a West African State: A Study of the Modernization Process in Sierra Leone* (Cambridge: Harvard University Press, 1966).

groups through migration into both urban and rural areas since Kikuyu had migrated to the Rift Valley farms to work the lands of white farmers.

Land continued to be a divisive feature among Kenya's people after independence. The distribution of former white-held land was a major aim of the independent Kenyan Government; tribal conflict was focused on land issues. In the towns of the Rift Valley, Western Province, and in Mombasa, migration of Kikuyu and Luo especially produced fears of domination by newcomers over the indigenous inhabitants of the areas surrounding the towns. Moreover, as migrant workers returned to their home areas after a spell in the towns or the rural estates, tribal feelings were often heightened in the homeland, or created for the first time as stories of conflict were told and stereotypes developed. Kikuyu sensitivities had been particularly engaged when thousands of Kikuyu were forcibly repatriated from the white highlands during Mau Mau.

The spur to the formation of KADU had been minority tribes' fear of Luo and Kikuyu domination which crystallized around the land issue in the Rift Valley where the Kalenjin Political Alliance and similar tribal associations became the constituent elements of KADU. Town-based associations like the Nakuru African Progressive Party played an analogous role.

It was not surprising that Kikuyu became the focus of discontent in Kenya because of Kikuyu domination of critical Cabinet posts and the top of the Government itself. The inner core of the Cabinet has been Kikuyu but the extent of Kikuyu domination of the country may have been exaggerated.

An early study of the Kenyan elite (Tables VIII, IX) based on a Who's Who of income, position, elected or appointed office, shows a disproportionate number of Kikuyu, especially in the Civil Service. But it also shows a disproportionately large number of Luhya and minority tribal representation too.[4]

While Kikuyu appointments were frequently made to the Civil Service, there is no evidence that Kikuyus have been vastly overrepresented in it if their educational advantages are taken into account.[5]

It is difficult to know if Kikuyu dominance of the Civil Service has grown. Certainly non-Kikuyu think it has and Government has made its Staff List a restricted document so that MPs can no longer note on the floor of the National Assembly the large number of Kikuyu names in the ranks of the Civil Service. The Kenyatta Govern-

[4] Even Kikuyu and Luo seem to feel that smaller tribes are relatively neglected by Government. In a survey carried out by Donald Rothchild ("Ethnic Inequalities"), based on 653 completed questionnaires in 1966, 61 percent of the Kikuyus and 55 percent of the Luos surveyed stated that smaller tribes were neglected in the field of education. Figures rose to 68 percent of the Luhyas and 84 percent of the Kisiis surveyed. To feel this is not to agree that *favoritism* has been shown to dominant tribes.

[5] One study of the Kenya elite concluded that "the singularly most striking feature of the Kenya elite is the pre-eminence of the Kikuyu" (Michael Chaput and Ladislav Venys, *A Survey of the Kenya Elite*, Maxwell Graduate School of Citizenship and Public Affairs, Program of Eastern African Studies, Syracuse University, Occasional Paper No. 25, p. 9). It is true that Kikuyu are disproportionately represented as inhabitants of Nairobi; it is true that they are better educated and have more members in voluntary associations. Chaput and Venys, however, counted the Embu and Meru in with the Kikuyu because they are culturally and linguistically related. Embu and Meru together are almost 30 percent as large as Kikuyu. Chaput and Venys' figures do not show a disproportionate number of Kikuyu in local government participation, or trade union membership (where there are more Luos), or elected government positions.

TABLE VIII
KENYA ELITE BY TRIBAL GROUP

Tribe	Percent of Population	Percent of Elite
Kikuyu	19.5	23
Luo	14.4	19
Luhya	12.5	19
Kamba	11.7	6
Meru	6.9	2
Kisii	4.9	3
Embu	3.9	1
Kipsigis	3	2
Nandi	2.2	1
others (less than 3%)	16.1	22
stated Tanganyikan	–	2
Total	100	100
Base	5,251,120	457

SOURCE: All figures from Gordon Wilson, "The African Elite," in Diamond and Burke, *Transformation of East Africa*, pp. 445, 448. Their figures in column I do not add to 100 percent.

NOTE: The data is based on surveys done for *Who's Who in East Africa, 1963-64* (Nairobi: Marco Surveys, LTD, 1964). Respondents were preselected. There were three criteria for selection. Income of £1,000 per annum was one cut-off point. Position held by a respondent could qualify him even if he did not have the requisite income; for example, the mayor of a local town qualified. The third criterion was the power position of the post occupied. All elected or appointed members of central and regional governments qualified regardless of other factors, as did African professionals. There were 60 women out of 1423 interviews. The authors used 1948 census data and assumed a proportionate rate of increase among tribes over time for the population figures. Kikuyus have grown slightly faster than the proportionate rate according to the 1969 census.

TABLE IX

PROFESSION AND TRIBE IN KENYA

Tribe	Civil Servants (percent)	Elected or Appointed Representatives (percent)	Nongovernmental Professionals (percent)
Kikuyu	29	17	27
Embu	–	3	1
Meru	1	4	2
Luo	23	12	26
Taveta	–	–	–
Masai	1	4	1
Nandi	2	1	–
Wakamba	9	6	5
Kipsigis	2	3	1
Luhya	20	13	25
Iteso	1	–	–
Taita	2	2	–
Non-Somali N.F.D.	–	2	–
Kisii	1	5	–
Kalenjin	1	9	–
Coast	4	12	7
stated Kenyan others	–	2	–
Tanganyika tribe	2	–	3
not stated	2	5	2
Total	100	100	100
Base	123	190	183

SOURCE: All figures from Wilson, "The African Elite," pp. 445, 448, based largely on surveys done in 1963-64. I have retitled the Table.

ment has been committed to the game of tribal representation both in the higher Civil Service and in the Cabinet.

After Tom Mboya's assassination, President Kenyatta demonstrated his continued commitment to tribal representation by appointing two Luos, Odero-Jowi and R. Ouko, to his Cabinet at a time when Luos as a community were opposing him. Every tribe with better than 2 percent of the population has had a Minister or Junior Minister.[6] There are large numbers of Junior Ministers in the Kenya Cabinet: 36. Moreover, the Rift Valley Province which is inhabited by smaller tribes had 40 percent of the votes at the KANU Limuru Conference in 1966. The Rift Valley has been overrepresented in terms of seats per inhabitant in the new Parliament.[7] The alliance between Kenyatta and Moi, Vice President of Kenya and leader of the Rift Valley, has guaranteed them voting dominance in KANU and in Parliament.

If Kikuyu leaders have favored Kikuyu frequently, at least one reason is that their own base of support constitutes a problem for them. The problem for the Kikuyu leadership of Kenya is that Kikuyu have by no means been a homogenous community. There have been religious splits among Kikuyu and territorial ones as well. People define themselves as coming from one or another Kikuyu areas. Districts have different levels of development and locational loyalties have become mixed with developmental differences. We can see income and educational variations by districts in Tables x, xi below.

[6] Jay E. Hakes, "The Recruitment of Political Leaders in the National Assembly of Kenya," unpublished paper. Four former KPU MPs were also in this new Cabinet after the 1969 elections.

[7] The Rift Valley had 37 seats for a population of 2.2 million, whereas Nyanza had 23 seats for 2.1 million, Central Province had 21 seats for 1.7 million, and Eastern had 27 seats for 1.9 million.

TABLE X

INCOME IN CENTRAL PROVINCE, 1963-64

Nos. of Households	*Fort Hall (Muran'ga) (percent)*	*Kiambu (percent)*	*Nyeri (percent)*	*Embu (percent)*	*Meru (percent)*	*All Districts (percent)*
with income under $135 per year	39.7	26.9	7.9	64.7	57.7	41.5
with income over $350 per year	13.0	27.4	26.0	not given	not given	not given

SOURCE: *Economic Survey of Central Province, 1963-64* (Nairobi: Statistics Division, Ministry of Economic Planning and Development, 1968), p. 39, TABLE 52.

NOTE: A study of two cooperative societies in different locations but both within Kirinyaga District shows large differences in per capita income. See Edward Karanja, "A Case Study of Two Cooperatives in Kirinyaga District," IDS Staff Paper No. 62, Nairobi, February 1972.

TABLE XI

EDUCATION IN CENTRAL PROVINCE, 1963-64

	Fort Hall Muran'ga (percent)	Kiambu (percent)	Nyeri (percent)	Embu (percent)	Meru (percent)	All Districts (percent)
Males illiterate	33.0	31.1	41.6	47.0	53.7	41.5
Females illiterate	55.3	51.6	50.4	82.3	78.9	64.3
Standard IV or higher education for males	37.6	37.9	33.9	29.1	19.5	31.3

SOURCE: *Economic Survey of Central Province, 1963-64*, p. 12, TABLE 14.

In Thika town, for example, which is close to Nairobi and itself a growing industrial center, there has been migration of Kikuyu from the Kiambu areas of Kikuyuland which is the most advanced area educationally and is closest to Nairobi. It is also the place where the major political figures around President Kenyatta are from. There has been friction between Kiambu Kikuyu in Thika and Kikuyus who have migrated from Muran'ga district. This friction has been expressed in conflict over local elections, struggle for jobs, trade union elections. Moreover, Muran'ga has felt itself to be relatively neglected by Government. When the Kenya National Trade Corporation was giving out franchises which awarded distribution rights for certain commodities, there were claims among Kikuyu from Nyeri and Muran'ga that Kiambu Kikuyu were favored. There was a partially successful attempt to have franchisers be from their own districts.[8]

There have been clan distinctions among Kikuyu.[9] And, while Mau Mau bound elements of the Kikuyu community more closely together, it also widened fissures and created new conflicts between Loyalists and Mau Mau supporters. Economic differences were tied up with Mau Mau too. As Sorrenson has pointed out, land consolidation accelerated the development of a landless class which had been forming even before the 1950s.[10] Not all those who supported Mau Mau in the rural areas were landless or were the jobless from the towns. Mau Mau also recruited better educated people in the towns and

[8] From interviews with officials of the Ministry of Trade and provincial administrators in Nyeri town and district.

[9] For a discussion of Kikuyu kinship system see Jomo Kenyatta, *Facing Mt. Kenya* (London: Mercury Books, 1961).

[10] Sorrenson, *op.cit.*, p. 227.

trade unionists, too. Some leaders had been abroad in the armed forces like General China (Itote) and Bildad Kaggia. But most of the forest fighters were illiterate and poor. The Mau Mau experience itself created conflicts as family feuds hardened or formed over the question of terrorism.

Confronted with splits in the Kikuyu community, Kenyatta had first to solidify his base. For him, the critical problems posed were as much the divisions *among* Kikuyu as the ethnic/economic tensions *between* Kikuyus and others. The social and economic bases for splits among Kikuyu in the 1950s were to widen in the 1960s. Population grew fastest among Kikuyu.[11] In absolute and relative numbers more Kikuyu were upwardly mobile as they took over from Asian traders, purchased land from other tribes either alone or in consortiums and cooperatives, moved into the former white farms, began to move into foreign commercial and industrial enterprises as managers, and increasingly moved into the officer corps.[12] At the same time, Kikuyu were becoming landless and unemployed in large numbers.

In many new African states, tribal tension was great

[11] The 1962 census gave the figure 19.2 percent Kikuyu out of the total population. In 1969 there were 2,201,632 Kikuyu out of 10,942,705 Kenyans. In percentage terms Kikuyu had moved to more than 20 percent.

[12] In 1962, Kikuyus had been underrepresented in the police and army officer corps. There had been a deliberate colonial policy not to recruit Kikuyu for army or police. By 1966, almost 23 percent of the officers in the army were Kikuyu. By 1967, there were as many Kikuyu as the once dominant Kamba. A General Service Unit had been created as a riot control force which was largely Kikuyu-officered. For figures on tribal balance within the Kenya officer corps see J. M. Lee, *African Armies and Civil Order* (London: Chatto and Windus, 1969), p. 110.

after independence because the opportunities that opened up as Africans moved into high positions in the Civil Service, the military, and educational institutions were seen as being "once and for all." Control of critical institutions in society gave tribal groups great advantages that could then be built-in subsequently. In Kenya, this process took place, too, but it was even more fraught with tension and consequence because Kenya had an extensive white settlement on the land and because it shared with its East African neighbors a large Asian[13] commercial sector and its industry was dominated by Europeans. In Kenya, however, the pockets of commerce and industry were larger than elsewhere in East Africa because Kenya was more economically developed. So far, Africanization has meant more the opening up to Africans of trade and small business than industry. Asians were vulnerable politically and economically, more so than Europeans in technical and managerial positions who could easily leave Kenya. Threatening Europeans' managerial and industrial position would mean jeopardizing new inflows of foreign aid and private investment. Asians, however, posed no such problem. Africanization of managerial posts in large firms has taken place for personnel officers, public relations officers, and salesmen, and Africans have been given high-sounding titles. But managerial control has been retained by expatriates.[14]

[13] In East Africa the term "Asians" is used as an umbrella to cover people of Indian, Pakistani, Goan, sometimes Arab extraction. There are many subgroups, e.g., Hindu or Muslim, Ismaili, etc.

[14] A discussion of Africanization of managerial positions can be found in *The Report of the Select Committee to Investigate into Possibilities of Africanization in All Fields* (with Minutes), Nairobi, mimeograph, 1969. This report claimed that the Gov-

While Kenyan Africans in general were assumed to want the elimination of racial stratification generated by Asian control of certain economic sectors, observers have usually agreed that it was in the urban and peri-urban areas and specifically among elites that the strongest demands for Africanization came.[15] Okumu argued that the phenomenon of uneven development was most keenly felt by elites who consciously competed for scarce resources in society and that this competition was sharpest among more advanced tribes. The situation was aggravated by an educational system which continued to produce manpower faster than jobs could be created.[16] Rothchild's surveys among Africans conducted in 1966, showed, however, that the pressures for take-over of Asian business were generated by older, less educated males.[17] Among the tribes, Luo much less strongly felt the need for an aggressive Africanization policy than Kikuyu, Kamba, and Luhya, perhaps because Luo were less able to benefit from such a strategy. For by the time Africanization was being implemented in the mid-1960s through a loan and licensing program, Kikuyu especially had already made inroads into Asian trade. Indeed, Kikuyu had become themselves the targets of several town coun-

---

ernment was itself lagging on Africanizing the posts of Personal Secretaries because Ministers and Permanent Secretaries felt expatriates were more trustworthy and better qualified.

[15] See Donald Rothchild, "Kenya's Africanization Program: Priorities of Development and Equity," *American Political Science Review*, Vol. 64, No. 3 (September 1970), p. 738, and John Okumu, "The Problem of Tribalism in Kenya."

[16] Okumu, p. 15.

[17] Rothchild, p. 740. Rothchild's data also showed that a majority of all respondents felt that immigrant communities had helped to develop Kenya—a bare majority with regard to Asians, an overwhelming one with respect to Europeans.

cils in the Rift Valley who evicted Kikuyu traders when their licenses expired.[18]

Government's own policy toward Asians has in fact been a stop-go one, tightening restrictions on trade possibilities, then slackening off, only to limit Asian trade again shortly.[19] Government has feared that the economy will be harmed by trade contractions if it tightens the screws too quickly. Moreover, some elements of the Kenyan elite have also been moderate in their enthusiasm over rapid Africanization of trade. Civil Service heads of districts and provinces feared that rapid Africanization might lead to short run problems in supply of commodities and consequent rise in prices.[20] Their immediate concern was how farmers would react to higher prices and how development of rural areas would proceed if supply problems arose. At the same time that provincial and district commissioners voiced these concerns, trade unionists and Members of Parliament pushed hard for speedier Africanization.[21] The civil servants felt pressure from MPs directly and also from local politicians who

[18] Murray, "Succession Prospects."

[19] The major vehicles for limitation have been the Immigration Act, 1967, by which work permits can be refused to noncitizens, and the Trade Licensing Act of 1967 (Act No. 33) which empowers the Minister of Commerce to restrict non-citizen trade by refusal to grant licenses. In fact, the act has been applied at times to Asians who adopted Kenyan citizenship, although rectifications of injustices have been made to citizens too. For a discussion of the citizenship question in Kenya see Donald Rothchild, "Kenya's Minorities and the African Crises over Citizenship," *Race*, Vol. 9, No. 4 (1968), pp. 421-437.

[20] Interviews carried out in Nyeri and Embu Districts in 1968-69.

[21] Rothchild, "Kenya's Africanization Program," p. 741.

supported individuals for loans and licenses.[22] Loan boards were created which had appointees from the Ministry of Commerce and from the county councils. There were also special statutory boards for liquor licensing and transport licensing. Here too politicians supported individuals who asked for their intercession.

My own interviews in Nyeri and Embu districts led to the conclusion that the major force for pressure to Africanize and to intervene in the loan and licensing process was better-off farmers who split their trade and

[22] The regulations on trade licensing were complicated and a number of administrative bodies came into play. Provincial and district trade officers were appointed as agents of the Ministry of Commerce in the field. In theory, the process of granting licenses was highly centralized with all reports going back to Nairobi. Central Government licenses superseded town and county council ones. Yet the town councils and county councils could give local licenses and also give plots for markets. And in some cases, traders were given quit notices without a municipal council's knowledge. This happened in Kisumu. (See *Daily Nation*, June 21, 1969, p. 14.) The Ministry of Commerce acted on advice of the provincial trade officer but since the issue was politically loaded, district and provincial commissioners sometimes became involved. The Ministry of Commerce was also supposed to process all requests to the Kenya National Trading Corporation and the Industrial and Commercial Development Corporation. In practice, KNTC gave licenses without ministerial knowledge while ICDC did not. For a discussion of administrative arrangements within the Ministry of Commerce see Ministry of Commerce and Industry Note No. 1/69, Nairobi, 1969. Also see Frank Mitchell and Henry Bienen, "Study of the Efficiency and Organization of Distribution," IDS Staff Paper No. 38, Nairobi, February 10, 1969. For an outline of a study on the KNTC see J. J. Bucknall, "The Role of State Trading in Kenya with Special Reference to the Kenya National Trading Corp." IDS Staff Paper No. 49, Nairobi, October 1969.

farming activities. These were men who spent part time trading in the town or market center and were back on their farms part of the week. They would also buy trade premises and had access to county council members and MPS.

Africanization of trade has been an issue closely followed in the press and as new African traders are announced in the major towns and market locations the press reports on it. Government has insisted that the granting of trade licenses and loans will not be based on tribal or sectional interests.[23] There is general feeling in Kenya that trade loans and licenses are going disproportionately to Kikuyu.[24]

Information is available on industrial loans to businessmen through the work of Peter Marris and Anthony Somerset. Marris and Somerset surveyed businessmen whom the Industrial and Commercial Development Cor-

[23] Statement of the Minister for Commerce and Industry, Mwai Kibaki, *East African Standard*, June 17, 1969.

[24] In some Kikuyu districts, wholesale and retail trade is now said to be in African hands. See statement of K. Mukiri, Chairman of the Kiambu County Council, *East African Standard*, June 5, 1969. Loans for traders have been reported in the past by district. Thus Kikuyu may have received loans outside their home districts. In 1965, less than $100,000 was reported lent under a small loans scheme from district joint development boards and about $500,000 more was lent by the ICDC. Central Province and Nairobi together received about a third of the total. See Republic of Kenya, The National Assembly, House of Representatives, *Official Report*, Vol. 13, Part II, Fourth Session, June 7, 1965. The 1967 figures as reported do not show any totals for Central Province. These figures can be found in Cherry Gertzel, Maure Goldschmidt, Donald Rothchild, eds., *Government and Politics in Kenya* (Nairobi: East African Publishing House, 1969).

poration (ICDC) had given loans to.[25] These businessmen came from a range of backgrounds; 60 percent were children of peasant farmers and the rest were sons of craftsmen, shopkeepers, schoolteachers, junior government officers, clergy. The sons of peasants were 25 percent from prosperous farmers; 22 percent from average ones; and 14 percent from poor ones. The businessmen had been, prior to going into the business for which they received a loan, in a variety of occupations including over 10 percent who had been unemployed.[26]

Interestingly, the businessmen had characteristically been active in the Kenya Independence struggle.

> But as an African government came to power, and their own part in political life began to seem less meaningful, they transferred their patriotism to entrepreneurship. Business became a substitute for both administrative influence and political leadership, where lack of educational sophistication was less of a drawback.[27]

Marris and Somerset tell us that the businessmen tended to limit their involvement in politics; a number refused to stand for office. But they were not people without political interests or connections. While 9 percent took part in local party committees and 10 percent were town or county councillors, most were not so visible in politics. Marris and Somerset state that the ICDC-supported businessmen saw themselves as economic men as

[25] Peter Marris and Anthony Somerset, *African Businessmen* (London: Routledge and Kegan Paul, 1971). Also see Peter Marris, "The Social Barriers to African Entrepreneurship," *Journal of Development Studies*, Vol. 15, No. 1 (October 1968), pp. 29-39.

[26] Marris and Somerset, *African Businessmen*, pp. 59, 62.

[27] *Ibid.*, p. 67.

party politics changed and manipulation of Government rather than mass movement anti-regime politics governed.[28] Yet, 25 percent of the businessmen had facilitated the negotiation of their ICDC loan by political contacts. They did not get more money or better terms but they did get money more quickly.[29] These men did not want to play an overt role in factional politics and probably they are people who would try to make their peace with dominant factions; but they certainly are not cut off from politics.

Once again the ethnic composition of ICDC-supported businessmen is striking. Kikuyu received loans at two or three times what their number would justify.[30] The senior staff of ICDC was Kikuyu but Marris and Somerset found that the proportions could not be attributed to favoritism. Undoubtedly, it is not so perceived by non-Kikuyu in Kenya.

Kikuyu domination of entrepreneurial activities creates ethnic friction within Kenya but it also opens up social mobility within Kikuyu society. Indeed, Marris and Somerset stress that the Kikuyu entrepreneurs were people often educationally thwarted and occupationally frustrated. Marris could find no correspondence between education and business success.[31] It would appear that

[28] *Ibid.*, p. 68. [29] *Ibid.*, p. 69.

[30] *Ibid.*, p. 71. Kikuyu with 19 percent of the male population (based on 1962 census) received 64 percent of industry loans and 44 percent of commerce loans from ICDC up to April 1966. Luo with 14 percent of the male population had 12 percent and 11 percent industry and commerce loans.

[31] Marris, "Social Barriers." An outline of a study in progress is Jasper A. Okelo, "Know-How and Success in Retail—A Case Study of Traders in River Road," IDS Staff Paper No. 69, Nairobi, April 1970; also see Audun Sandberg, "Generation Conflict and Entrepreneurship in Meru," IDS Staff Paper No. 52, Nairobi, December 1969.

for a not large number of Kikuyu, Africanization of business provides for movement out of semiskilled occupations and farming. It is also true that "the big men," Africans who have achieved wealth through private enterprise or have used politics to move into directorships, are largely but not exclusively Kikuyu.[32] Africans not clearly identified as political people who are prominent in business are largely Kikuyu.

Ethnic considerations are perceived as critical for the way individuals and social groups deal with each other and with Government.

Ross's sample of Nairobi residents shows that a large percentage considers tribalism to be a serious problem in Kenya.

Nairobi is not representative of urban Kenya much less all of Kenya. But there is little doubt that ethnicity retains its salience in rural areas as well as urban ones although most of the survey data have been gathered from urban and peri-urban areas.[33] Ethnicity in the towns

[32] Oginga Odinga, the Luo leader, achieved wealth through his leadership of a Luo commercial corporation. For African participation in high industry see *Who Controls Industry in Kenya* (Nairobi: East African Publishing House, 1968).

[33] There is an extensive literature on urban ethnicity in Africa. If scholars now seem agreed that tribalism in the towns ". . . is a category of interaction within a wider urban system" (Judith Hanna and William John Hanna, *Urban Politics in Black Africa* [New York: Free Press, 1971], p. 123), they are by no means agreed on how that interaction takes place. For a bibliographical essay on urban ethnicity in Africa see *ibid.*, pp. 105-143. For two particularly interesting discussions see Immanuel Wallerstein, "Ethnicity and National Integration in West Africa," originally published in *Cahiers d'Etudes Africaines*, Vol. 1, No. 3 (1960), pp. 129-139 and widely reprinted, where Wallerstein discusses ethnic groups in terms of urban social situations rather than as traditional groups. Also see Max Gluckman, "Tribalism

TABLE XII

Degree of Seriousness of Government Officials and
Politicians Doing Special Favors for Relatives and
Close Friends, and Tribalism in Nairobi Today

	How serious is the problem of politicians doing special favors for relatives and close friends? *(percent)*	How serious a problem do you think tribalism is in Nairobi today? *(percent)*
Very serious	55	50
Serious	18	20
Not important	11	14
Don't know	16	16
	100	100
Sample size	491	497

SOURCE: Ross, *op.cit.*, pp. 272-73.

is also evident from elections. Moreover, ethnic conflict
is not just an elite phenomenon. Since rural-urban areas
can be thought of as one network rather than as discon-
tinuous living spaces in Kenya, ethnic tensions are
brought from towns to rural areas. And since land has
been such a major issue between tribal groups, there is
good reason to believe that ethnic considerations are at
least as important for support or nonsupport of Government in the rural areas.

in Modern British Central Africa," *Cahiers d'Etudes Africaines*,
Vol. I (1960), pp. 55-70, who argued that tribal influences from
outside the towns continued to operate in town milieus but
insisted that common interests of groups in the towns overrode
tribal interests, although new associations might be cast in tribal
terms.

Whether rural data would show that ethnicity is the best predictor of an individual's attitudes toward Government, as Ross's data show for Nairobi among major tribal groups, is an open question.[34] The one clear indication that does exist is overwhelming support for the KPU in Luo areas in 1966. It is evident, however, that tribal support is mediated through ethnic commitment to factions led by prominent individuals. Thus part of the Kamba area also supported the KPU in the Little General Election in 1966, and individuals, as we noted earlier, have been able to swing their groups behind a party or party faction. Daniel Moi, Ronald Ngala, and Paul Ngei were able to do this when they joined KANU.

We also know that land issues have been critical in Kenyan politics. As noted earlier, KADU was formed in opposition to KANU in large part because both Rift Valley and Coastal minority tribes feared encroachments on their land. The major land resettlement that took place after independence can be seen as a bargain struck between Kikuyu and Rift Valley leaders. It is an unstable bar-

[34] Marc Howard Ross, "Grassroots in the City, Political Participation and Alienation in Nairobi after Independence," pp. 262-263. Kikuyus have more favorable attitudes to Government while Luos have least and Kamba are in between in Nairobi. Kikuyus perceive the greatest improvement in living conditions since independence and Luos the least. Ross's study of participation in Nairobi shows that when asked to name their closest friends, respondents from the largest tribes, Kikuyu, Luo, Kamba, and Luhya, name their own tribesmen by better than 80 percent for all the four tribes. Moreover, Ross's data show that having their own tribesmen as best friends and making ethnic political identifications of choice of leaders is unrelated to education, income, or any measures used for length of residence in the city, although individuals with a higher education and income do operate in larger spheres of social interaction in selecting secondary friends.

gain at best, but it is the base for the present regime's power and it is the core of the factional alliance system in KANU. Kikuyus are already moving out from their initial settlement areas and chafing at governmental restraints. For while Kikuyus received some 45 percent of the land in the Million Acre Scheme[35] of resettlement, thousands of Kikuyu farm laborers were displaced by Kalenjin-speaking and Kisii peoples who were resettled on the former Rift Valley European farms.

Originally, it was expected that laborers who had worked on European farms would receive priority for resettlement on the land they worked. In practice, land was frequently given in tribal settlements, and members of a different tribe were removed. Only those who had worked for four or more years were permitted to stay and thus about 40 percent of the migrant laborers got land. The rest had to move.[36] It was often Kalenjin and Kisii, rather than Kikuyu, who acquired the most fertile land, and they received the most land in relation to population and needs.[37] The less developed tribes conceived

[35] John Harbeson, "Land Reforms and Politics in Kenya," *Journal of Modern African Studies*, Vol. 9, No. 2 (August 1971), p. 243. There are many studies of Kenya's land transfer program. Among them are: Barbara Herz, *"Land Reform in Kenya,"* AID Spring Review Country Paper, June 1970; A. W. Seidman, "The Agricultural Revolution," *East Africa Journal*, Vol. 8, No. 8 (August 1970), pp. 21-36; Leys, "Politics in Kenya," and William J. Barber, "Land Reform and Economic Change Among African Farmers in Kenya," *Economic Development and Cultural Change*, Vol. 14, No. 1 (October 1970), pp. 6-24. I have very much benefited from reading Gary Wasserman's unpublished work on land resettlement.

[36] Seidman, "The Agricultural Revolution," p. 25.

[37] Aaron Segal, "The Politics of Land in East Africa," *Africa Report*, Vol. 12, No. 4 (April 1967), pp. 49-50. Segal argues that the switch of Kalenjin support to KANU, symbolized by

of consolidation and titling of land, which had largely been carried out before independence in Central Province, as a means of preventing landless Kikuyu from encroaching on their lands.

It is clear that land issues heightened tribal tensions in rural areas and that tribal tensions have been extremely serious in rural and urban Kenya. I argue below that the threat to the present regime in Kenya, however, is not most immediately that of tribal conflict. Nor is it a threat from a coalition of have-nots and disaffected economic groups in Kenya. Rather, it is fissures in the regime's own base, its Kikuyu core constituency, that are most dangerous for the regime. The policies that have been devised by Government, the kinds of benefits Government provides to groups, keep in focus the problems of cleavage and consensus among Kikuyu in the context of the clear economic trends which exist in Kenya.

B. CLASS POLITICS IN THE TOWNS?

Discussions of the possibilities of class-based politics in developing countries often center on the rapid urbanization which is taking place. Traditional Marxist analyses concentrated on the growth of a stable working class based on industry in the cities or on enclaves of mining industry or transport which have existed in various developing countries. The cities of the Third World, however, have expanded much more rapidly than employment opportunities have expanded and employed workers have appeared as a priviledged group in their

---

Daniel Arap Moi's becoming Vice President of Kenya after having been a KADU leader, was based on the fulfillment of the promise of a good land deal. Luo, on the other hand, have been left out of the land settlement.

countries. They usually have wanted higher wages rather than demanded expanded opportunities for new entrants into the working class. Workers in trade unions have not shown much revolutionary potential in Africa although they have been class or, more accurately, occupation-oriented in the sense that they have organized to defend their economic privileges. Therefore, analysts who have tried to assess the potential for revolutionary change have shifted their attention to two large categories: urban marginals—those who are unemployed or who are intermittently employed and who have swelled the fast-growing cities—and the rural poor.[38]

Kenya has its share of urban marginals. The towns are growing rapidly, although there are only two cities with more than a quarter of a million people. Nairobi has more than half a million and Mombasa more than a quarter of a million. Unemployment and the strain on budgets of providing more social services to the towns are seen to be problems by Government. Increasingly, Government spokesmen espouse a back-to-the-land ideology, preach against idlers and the vices of the towns, and as I shall show, devote important resources to the rural areas. But the cities and towns of Kenya are not where a class-based political action *against* the regime is going to take place.

Trade unions in Kenya have been brought into the ruling structure. Their leaders play the game of shifting

[38] Joan Nelson has examined the literature on urban marginals in "The Urban Poor: Disruption or Political Integration in Third World Cities," *World Politics*, Vol. 22 (April 1970), pp. 393-414 and in her *Migrants, Urban Poverty and Instability in Developing Nations*, Harvard University Center of International Affairs, Occasional Paper, Vol. 22, 1968. Fanon, *op.cit.*, has emphasized the revolutionary potential of poor peasants.

alliances and coalitions within KANU. The unions have been brought under Government control through a process of co-optation together with the enacting of legislation to control trade union elections and activities. Workers with jobs are fearful of losing them by opposing already established union leaders.[39] Employed workers are a "have" element in the society.

The obstacles to political action among the urban poor have been well demonstrated.[40] They have unstable residences, low membership rates in voluntary associations, low trust in leaders, lack of funds, few meeting places or contacts, ethnic cleavages. Moreover, they are easily coerced, and do not easily see the relationship of collective acts to individual self-interest or have faith in their feasibility. Political organizations that might help people make these connections have not existed in Kenya.[41] The trade unions have not acted to fashion political ties among the urban poor and the KPU was not organized at the grass roots in the towns. Nor were its dissident activities given much leeway by the Government. While there is a great deal of migration from rural areas to the towns and then migration back to rural areas, urban discontent does not get expressed as large-scale urban instability which is then exported back to rural areas.[42]

[39] The most thorough discussion of trade unions in Kenya can be found in the works of Sandbrook, cited above.

[40] See Nelson, "Urban Poor."

[41] For a study of the existence of such organizations in Lima and Santiago see Daniel Goldrich, "Political Organization and the Politicization of the Poblador," *Comparative Political Studies*, Vol. 3, No. 2 (July 1970), pp. 176-203.

[42] This occurred in late 19th and early 20th century Russia. Peasants newly arrived in the cities brought the grievances from the land with them. They lived and worked under the terrible conditions of Russian cities; some became organized there and

The lack of organization is a critical factor. One reason why it is difficult to organize the poor in towns is that a sizable proportion of them regard their stay in the city as temporary. While many city dwellers regard their stay as temporary, those who are poorest have fragile ties to the town. Those who are landless may try to survive in the city but they are often also those with lowest wages. They cannot sustain their ties to the rural areas on a steady basis since they do not have funds to make trips home. But they do not form a permanent dispossessed group in the towns either. If they continue to be without jobs, they have to return to the country to work on someone else's farm. One study of an urban sample stated that only about one-fifth of the informants were landless.[43] Those with and without land seem to care more about local politics in their home areas than the politics of the towns or even the wards in which they temporarily dwell. Another study of an urban sample of employed workers showed that 87 percent regularly remitted money to the rural areas. This was about 25 percent of the urban wage bill.[44]

Because there is so much back migration from town to rural areas, perhaps no clear-cut economic, social, and political divisions between rural and urban areas can be made in Kenya. So far, the pattern is not one of a radical urban element "infecting" the countryside despite the close ties that exist between town and countryside. Work-

returned to rural areas, bringing with them new urban grievances strengthened and formed by political organizations.

[43] Henry Rempel, John Harris, Michael P. Todaro, "Rural to Urban Labour Migration: A Tabulation of Responses to the Questionnaire Used in the Migration Survey," IDS Staff Paper No. 39, Nairobi, March 1970.

[44] George E. Johnson, "Notes on Wages, Employment and Income Distribution," IDS, Nairobi, 1971.

ers with low skills remain unorganized and passive in the towns.

Discontented people in the towns—that is the students, unemployed, low-wage workers—do not make easy bedfellows. Urban instability is not being exported by them to the countryside. What both rural and urban groups want is more jobs for people to migrate to. This is a shared interest but it does not provide the basis for a class politics in Kenya.

The great potential for eruption in Kenya is on the land. And it exists because more jobs cannot be created fast enough for the would-be migrants to the towns. Thus Government must come to grips with the tensions in the rural areas by formulating land and agricultural development policies. The following facts should make this clear.

Overwhelmingly, Kenyans live on the land and will continue to do so. The process of industrialization or development of tertiary services has not and will not proceed at a pace fast enough, given population rise, to begin to meet the problem of unemployment, despite the fact that output rose at above 6½ percent a year after 1964. In Kenya, as Rado puts it, for every person who leaves the labor force through natural causes there are almost three who enter it.[45]

> Furthermore, as only one person in four of the present labor force is in wage employment of some kind, there are, on the average, 12 new entrants into the labor force for every job that arises through natural wastage. Hence, resources that could be used to raise the levels of living of the individual must be used, in part, to maintain levels already reached, but for more people.[46]

[45] Emil Rado, "Employment, Incomes Policy: Kenya's New Development Plan," *East Africa Journal*, Vol. 8, No. 3 (March 1970), p. 13.
[46] *Ibid.*

Estimated wage employment increased by only 16 percent or 3.8 percent per annum which was less than half the rate of output increase.[47]

Even if employment in the modern sector expands at 4.5 percent a year from 1970 to 1974, only 134,000 new jobs get created. Nearly 80 percent of the additional labor force would have to be absorbed in the rural sector, either as employees or as self-employed on farms and other enterprises.[48] Leys sees the number that will have to be supported on the land as between one and two million people between 1970 and 1980, over and above those who are to be employed as rural workers. We are talking about a society in which population growth is now thought to be 3.3 percent a year and where 55 percent of the population was under 15 in 1969.[49]

Thus most of Kenya's people will continue to live on the land. It is in the rural areas where class conflict threatens the regime. The critical issues for Government have been land issues from the start of Kenya's existence as an independent state. And the critical areas of economic differentiation on the land are the Kikuyu ones.

It has been the Kikuyu leaders—especially Kaggia, who have raised the specter of class warfare in Kenya— that have been so dangerous to the regime and it has

[47] *Ibid.* Rado thinks that even this rise in employment may be overstated because it is based partially on surveys of rural wage employment rather than enumerated employment figures. Ghai, *op.cit.*, p. 6, on the other hand, sees wage employment in the traditional sector (rural) expanding at over 8 percent per year and thus concludes that total employment growth may be understated.

[48] Dharam Ghai, "Employment Performance, Prospects and Policies in Kenya," *East Africa Journal*, Vol. 7, No. 11 (November 1970), p. 7.

[49] Leys, *Politics in Kenya*, p. 326.

TABLE XIII

Recorded Employment in the Modern Sector: 1960-69

	1960	1961	1962	1963	1964[a]	1965	1966	1967	1968	1969	Annual Percent Change 1964-69
Public Sector	161.4	167.0	167.0	159.5	182.0	188.2	200.4	212.1	221.9	237.6	5.5
Private Commerce & Industry	189.0	170.8	167.3	164.1	190.0[b]	190.8[b]	196.9	212.7	211.5	210.9	2.2
Agriculture & Forestry	271.8	252.0	245.5	215.7	201.1	212.4	188.1	172.7	173.0	178.7	−2.4
Total	622.2	589.8	579.8	539.3	573.1	581.4	585.4	597.5	606.4	627.2	3.5

SOURCES: *Statistical Abstract, 1965,* for 1960-63 figures; *Economic Survey, 1967,* for 1964-65 figures; *Economic Survey, 1970,* for 1966-69 figures.

[a] There is a break in the series owing to improved coverage in 1964, but this only affects employment in private commerce and industry.

[b] The figures published in the 1967 *Survey* have been adjusted to make them comparable to figures for 1966 and subsequent years as published in the 1970 *Survey.*

TABLE XIV

TOTAL WORK FORCE IN KENYA AS OF 1968

Wage Employment outside Agriculture	500,310
Wage Employment in Agriculture	556,600
Self-Employed in Agriculture	3,122,800
Self-Employed outside Agriculture	120,300

SOURCE: Leys, "Politics in Kenya," *op.cit.*, p. 311. Leys's source was *Development Plan, 1970-74*, TABLE 4.1.

TABLE XV

PROJECTED INCREASES IN POPULATION, LABOR FORCE, ADULT MALES

	1970	1971	1972	1973	1974	Total
Increase in population	359	371	383	396	409	1,918
Increase in labor force	126	130	134	139	143	672
Increase in male adults	82	85	88	91	94	440

SOURCE: Ghai, *op.cit.*, p. 7.

devoted great energy to defeat them. For them Kenyatta reserved the worst Kikuyu epithets, implying that they were not true Kikuyu and were traitors to the community and its values. The then Minister of Labour, Dr. Kiano, said: "We all come from humble beginnings. We are all related by blood, marriage, school ties, or political ties which give us national solidarity." As he warned thus against class warfare, he was speaking to the regime's greatest problem: splits in Kikuyu society that could be exploited by Kikuyu leaders, and he was speaking out of the regime's greatest fear.[50]

C. CLASS POLITICS ON THE LAND?

At independence, Kenya undertook a major land resettlement program which involved long and difficult negotiations between London, the Kenya Government, African nationalists, and white farmers. The settlement terms and Kenya's land programs have been criticized widely on the grounds that an elite of Kenyans benefited, that a British presence was maintained and further entrenched, that the colonial norms were preserved, and that a huge loan repayment burden was passed on to Kenyan farmers.[51] The nationalist movement was split not only between groups who emerged as KANU and KADU at the time of negotiations over the ground rules for the transition to an independent regime and the way that regime would look subsequently but also was split within what became KANU itself. Elements within KANU who broke with Kenyatta over the land question were led by Odinga and Kaggia.[52]

Odinga and Kaggia did not want Kenya to have to repay loans secured from Britain to buy out the settlers.

[50] *East African Standard*, October 10, 1967, as found in Gertzel, Goldschmidt, and Rothchild, *op.cit.*, p. 85.

[51] One of the best argued criticisms has been made in the unpublished work of Gary Wasserman. He sees the land transfer program as a successful attempt to continue the functioning of a political economy under an altered political hierarchy. One of the strong points of Wasserman's analysis is that he does not treat the European community as an economically and politically homogeneous one.

[52] Although only Kaggia criticized Kenyatta personally. Harbeson, *op.cit.*, p. 245.

They wanted a limit on the size of land holdings in the former European areas. They insisted on free land to the landless and a reduction of indebtedness of those who had settled on the Million Acre Scheme. These points became a major part of the program of the KPU.[53] But by no means was the discontent with Kenya's land policy restricted to opponents of the KANU Government who later resigned and joined the KPU. Many KANU backbenchers were to question Government's policy and especially the purchase of land by Ministers.[54]

Sorting out the actual settlement programs is hard enough much less trying to understand their whys and wherefores. A number of interwoven strands must be taken into account. Kenyatta's policy of reconciliation toward Europeans must be understood as a prerequisite for his policies within Kikuyuland. It was a British demand that white farmers be bought out by the Kenya Government which borrowed money from Britain for the buyout. For a regime in power, there were important things to be gained from maintaining ties with Britain. Kenya had great advantages in getting foreign aid and investment as compared to other African countries. These advantages were due to the infrastructure that had already been built, Kenya's relatively diversified economy, and the links between Europeans in Kenya and in Britain with outsiders in international banking and investment. On economic grounds, it could be argued persuasively

[53] The statement of the principles of the KPU was made in the *Wananchi Declaration: The Programme of the Kenya People's Union*, Nairobi, n.d. Debates in Parliament on the land question are reproduced in Gertzel, Goldschmidt, and Rothchild, *op.cit.*, pp. 129-136.

[54] For a particularly bitter debate see Republic of Kenya, The National Assembly Official Report, First Parliament, Vol. XIII, Fifth Session, Friday, October 6, 1967.

that it would be a mistake to do anything to threaten industrial and agricultural production which rested on a European presence.

In 1962-63 the new leaders were under tremendous pressures as independence approached. Land seizures were already taking place as Europeans abandoned farms, and lawlessness rose on the farms of those who remained. Large numbers of Kikuyu had remained without land or employment since they had been repatriated from the Rift Valley during the Emergency. And as detainees came out of detention camps there was a new pool of people pressuring for redress of grievances. Some Kikuyu threatened to go back into the forests to fight for a favorable land resettlement which meant free land to most of them. Land and Freedom armies reformed. At the same time, during 1960-63, the uncertainties surrounding independence led to economic contraction and a fall in employment of 14 percent.[55] Total gross domestic capital formation was lower in 1963 than in 1954 (at current prices).[56] A shaky Government needed to be propped up administratively by the remaining British personnel, economically by the hope of assistance, and politically by immediate programs that enabled the Government in the very short run to show that it was doing something for the landless, especially for Kikuyu landless.

In Kenya the nationalist leaders who hammered out the independence settlement with the British realized they were weak in terms of the tasks of rule and development. It was one thing to be able to dominate nationalist politics and another to survive under the pressures which

[55] Ghai, *op.cit.*, p. 5.

[56] V. P. Diejomaoh, "Tax Mobilization and Government Development Financing in Kenya," IDS Staff Paper No. 45, Nairobi, September 1969.

existed in Kenya. Kenyatta opposed the sweeping proposals for distributing land to the landless which were sponsored by Kaggia and Odinga because it ran against the grain of his own values. But more importantly, there was not enough land to accommodate demands and the Kenyatta regime could not have survived a rupture with the British over land take-overs. Kenya was not Guinea. Organizational weakness did not feed the fires of radicalism in the sense of refusing to accept the established system and its institutionalized procedures as the framework for further efforts in the direction of social change. Rather, the rulers' perception of their weakness accentuated movement toward accommodation with a number of former targets: colonial powers, Civil Service personnel, private economic interest groups, minority tribes. Staying in power was of overriding importance.[57] Of course, a political elite in Kenya stood to gain economically if it could step into the already ongoing economic system rather than dismantle it. This process did take place and it has been described above for Africanization of trade, commerce, and Civil Service.

What happened on the land, however, is less clear-cut. The first thing Government tried to do was to lance the boil of land seizures and growing lawlessness. It announced its intention to settle more than 30,000 families on what came to be called the Million Acre Scheme. Some called this a "counter-insurgency" program. The British Administrators clearly saw it as "letting the steam out of the kettle."[58] We could also call it Government

[57] For a discussion of deradicalization of African parties in power see Bienen, "Political Parties and Political Machines," pp. 211-212.

[58] Wasserman's research is very detailed on administrators' motives and actions. For one autobiographical statement see

responsiveness to crucial demands made on it. Resettlement was the clear priority at the time of independence and immediately afterward.

Government's major goal was to have a high visibility settlement on former European-held farms of people who were landless and had little money. At the same time, Government wanted to do two other things which were also important to it. It wanted to strengthen the group of middle-sized farmers on the land. This meant settling some farmers who could afford larger farms than the poorest category to be settled. And it wanted to reward its own powerful supporters. It thus devised a land program that would deal with three different groups at once: landless, small- to middle-sized farmers, and the political elite.

The Million Acre Scheme established different categories of land for resettlement. There were high-density schemes for peasants with little money which would establish an average family farm of around 27 acres. Lower-density schemes gave a farm size of about 37 acres. In theory, high-density schemes would cover 80 percent of the total area to be resettled and would provide for an income, over and above subsistence, of 25-75 pounds per annum per household. The low-density schemes would provide for incomes of 100 pounds per annum above subsistence. High-density schemes were to be settled by landless and unemployed who had to make a down payment of no more than six pounds.[59]

N. S. Carey Jones, *The Anatomy of Uhuru* (New York: Frederick Praeger, 1966), esp. pp. 135-178. Carey Jones was Permanent Secretary in the Ministry of Lands and Settlement and was critically involved in purchasing European farms for resettlement.

[59] There was a struggle over which administrative agencies would administer resettlement itself. KANU, KADU and the British

Low-density schemes were to recruit farmers with more farming experience and 100 pounds to put down. The pressures were such that some farmers were settled on high-density schemes where land and climate were not suitable for them. There was also a danger that land settlement might dispossess farm laborers in numbers equal to those being resettled.[60]

The Kenya Government was not completely sanguine about the economic benefits to be gained from resettlement.[61] It was clearly a political necessity with pressure on

---

in London differed over who would control the process. KADU wanted regional authorities to be able to reject settlers in order to protect minority tribes from central authorities that might impose Kikuyu settlers. There were administrative jurisdictional disputes between a Central Land Board and the Ministry of Settlements. In the end, the Ministry handled most of the resettlement. Farmers were actually selected by local committees working under the district commissioner. Candidates had to be unemployed landless but having some experience of agricultural work, and preference was to be given those who had worked estates. Approval had to be given by local settlement and agricultural officers and tribal authorities of the area. Edith Whetham, "Land Reform and Resettlement in Kenya," *East African Journal of Rural Development*, Vol. 1, No. 1 (January 1968), pp. 18-29.

[60] Despite all that has been written on Kenya's land programs, there is very little on the way individuals were chosen. Presumably it varied across districts. In one scheme (Mweiga), 40 percent of those chosen had no agricultural experience; 25 percent had worked on European farms (Wilson Nguyo, "Some Socio-Economic Aspects of Land Settlement in Kenya," Makerere Institute of Social Research Conference Papers, January 1967). For a detailed study of settlement schemes in Africa which deals extensively with Kenya see Robert Chambers, *Settlement Schemes in Tropical Africa* (New York: Frederick Praeger, 1969).

[61] Almost all studies of Kenyan resettlement schemes note that it is too early to say whether they are succeeding or not.

the Government from below by landless, and from above by the British and European farmers who wanted out of Kenya with repayment. These pressures continued and Government announced both an accelerated settlement program in 1963-64 and an expectation of settling people on another million acres. By 1969, more than 48,000 families had been settled on 1.37 million acres. Over 34,-000 families were settled on 135 settlements, of which 35 were low-density schemes with an average farm size of 15 hectares; 84 were high-density schemes with an average size of 11 hectares; and 16 were large-scale cooperatives, farms, or ranches.[62]

By 1970, Government clearly wanted to call a halt to massive resettlement.[63] Whereas three-quarters of all agricultural development funds went to land transfer programs in 1963-64, the percentage had fallen to 50 percent by 1968-69 and the 1970-74 Development Plan pro-

There is some evidence that the high density schemes have in some places done well. Nguyo, *op.cit.*

[62] Some 13,000 families were settled under a squatter scheme on 59,000 hectares of land or about 4.5 hectares per settler with 2.4 hectares of arable land per settler. These figures are from *Development Plan, 1970-74* (Nairobi: Government Printers, 1969), pp. 202, 207.

[63] Under the Stamp Land Purchase Programme agreed on between the British and Kenyan Governments 121 large-scale farms were to be bought from British farmers in the late 1960s. These farms were being purchased by the Agricultural Development Corporation which then leased them to citizen farmers with a view toward selling them if the tenants proved able to farm successfully. The ADC also kept farms to be run by itself (*Development Plan, 1970-74*, p. 209). Government stated its intention to settle 33,000 more squatters beyond the 13,000 that had been settled. It was dragging its feet on the program. *Ibid.*, p. 208.

jected only 22 percent for land transfers in 1970-74.[64] Government was very much aware of production problems on the settlement schemes. There had been substantial improvement in that the average value of production per hectare had increased from about $23 in 1964-65 to about $43 in 1966-67. The proportion of the output that was sold rather than retained on the farm rose from 30 percent in 1964-65 to 48 percent in 1966-67. Nonetheless, there was a high level of variability between performances on individual farms, and while the proportion of farms reaching the target income levels increased, it went from only 10 percent in 1964-65 to 17 percent in 1966-67. A high proportion of farmers incurred a cash deficit in all three years.[65] Moreover loan defaulting was widespread. At the end of 1966, 55.7 percent of the total 1.7 million pounds billed to settlers was in arrears and 23.1 percent had been in arrears for one year or longer. At the end of 1968, a total of 3.9 million pounds had been billed and 43.7 percent was in arrears.[66] The Kenyan Government had not given land in freehold to African settlers pending full loan repayment. Theoretically, settlers could be dismissed from their holdings, without benefit of court proceedings if they were in default of loans.[67] Threats have also been made to take back land if support for the Government was not forthcoming.[68] The *Development Plan for 1970-74* notes that some chronic defaulters have been evicted. In fact, few evictions have taken place and none of the politically power-

[64] *Development Plan, 1970-74*, p. 192.
[65] *Ibid.*, p. 203.   [66] *Ibid.*, p. 204.
[67] Harbeson, *op.cit.*, p. 249.
[68] Daniel Arap Moi, the Vice President, gave this warning in 1967. *Daily Nation* (Nairobi), September 6, 1967, as found in Good, *op.cit.*, p. 129, n. 50.

ful farmers who especially benefited from resettlement on large farms but who have sometimes been in arrears have been evicted.[69] These "big men" bought 259 farms of 100 acres each which were located around the farmhouses of former settler farms which were offered to Africans who could put down 500 pounds and 10 percent of the farm value. Originally, Government envisioned that the larger plots would have a target income of some 240 pounds and it called these "Yeoman Farms." In 1964, it moved to the 100 acre scheme and what became known as the "Z" plots built around established farmhouses. It was made explicit that these large plots would be bought by community leaders. Indeed, it was people with capital and political influence, which usually went together in Kenya, who bought plots, including some well-known leaders like Masinde Muliro, a former head of KADU and Chairman of the Maize Board.[70] Large farms were bought by high-level civil servants, some university lecturers, politicians, a few large farmers. It was estimated that by 1966 some 750 large farms averaging about 800 acres each

[69] Wasserman, *op.cit.*, reports that 158 recommendations for eviction went to the Sifting Committee in Parliament with 84 evictions resulting.

[70] Two fascinating interviews were carried out with two prominent politicians about their land holdings. Josiah Kariuki had been a former Mau Mau detainee and the author of a well-known book, *Mau Mau Detainee*. He had been one of Kenyatta's personal secretaries, an MP, and had become one of the richest Africans in Kenya. He owned more than 1,000 acres of land. Masinde Muliro, a former KADU head, and head of important Government boards owned more than 1,500 acres. Both defended their large land holdings. *Sunday Nation* (Nairobi), December 17, 1966 and November 6, 1966, reprinted in Gertzel, Goldschmidt, and Rothchild, *op.cit.*, pp. 78, 82-84.

were owned by Africans.[71] Many of these large farmers had gone into arrears on loans, too. Since so many of them were public figures, it was an awkward situation. And since so many public figures were absentee landlords, the performance of the "Z" plots left very much to be desired.[72]

Government had hoped that the maintenance of large farms would keep up the production of disposable farm output. Since it did not want to drive out all the remaining large European farmers, it was important to give them large African farmers as neighbors and allies. By creating various sized African farms, Government hoped to end the racial dualism of large European farms and African small holders and landless.[73] As Leys points out, the pattern of rural society that was envisioned was clear. It included a majority of independent small holders farming largely, but not exclusively, for subsistence; a group of middle farmers, and a smaller group of rich farmers or small capitalist farmers.[74] The Stolypin reforms were echoing in Kenya.[75]

Government did not think, however, that rural stability would be brought about by creating at best a few thousand large farmers. What Government meant by a middle class on the land and what the critics of its programs have understood by a middle class on the land

[71] Seidman, "The Agricultural Revolution," p. 206.

[72] Wasserman cites the Van Arcadie Mission of 1966 which complained that there had been no competitive bidding for farms under the "Z" schemes.

[73] Ruthenberg, *op.cit.*, p. 66.

[74] Leys, "Politics in Kenya."

[75] For a European settler's view of the desired rural development see Sir Michael Blundell, *So Rough A Wind* (London: Weidenfeld and Nicolson, 1964).

have been two different things. There has always been great confusion over the loosely used term "kulak."[76] Government hoped its stable base would be small farmers, not farmers with a hundred acres. In Government's view, even high-density scheme farmers would have a stake. The Kenya Government was serious about creating an alliance with its peasantry, especially in Central Province and the Rift Valley, but it was not counting on the political elite who "went back to the land" to do the job. It was counting on the small holders.

Government has counted on a rough equality in a peasant society and on personal ties to mitigate poverty and dampen hostilities. And it has counted on Kikuyu solidarity to submerge growing economic divisions which were accentuated by land consolidation and registration during the 1950s and perhaps further accentuated by resettlement programs and agricultural extension in the 1960s.

Government's hope that personal and clan ties in a peasant society will overlay income and land-holding distinctions is not chimerical. Economic differentiation proceeds in Kikuyuland but the political and social consequences of variations in land holdings and income are not clear. Relatively large income per capita is not necessarily positively correlated with relatively large land holdings for a household since larger households tend to have larger land holdings. Nor are income differences always and everywhere translated into significant life-style differences. Nonetheless, politicians who questioned Kikuyu

[76] The term gets applied to those who hire any labor in Tanzania; to various-sized farmers in Kenya. In the Soviet Union, a kulak was never defined by size of holding. In practice, a kulak could be anyone who opposed.

171

solidarity on the grounds that some Kikuyu had much more than others had to be dealt with harshly because they were plowing potentially fertile fields.

I have already mentioned the cleavages among Kikuyu by location, religion, position as Loyalist or freedom fighter during Mau Mau, factional groupings, and income. There are also strong grounds for Kikuyu solidarity. "We" and "they" distinctions can be fostered deliberately and oathing has taken place as an attempt to solidify community sentiments and bind people to common action. From the top comes the constant theme of reconciliation and Harambee. Past ties and activities during the Mau Mau Emergency still provide the basis for many factional groupings. But reconciliation among foes from Mau Mau days does appear to have taken place. Stockton reports from Nyeri which was an area of deep splits among Kikuyu:

> . . . of great immediate importance to the stability of present-day Kikuyu society, is the fact that there seems to have been a degree of reconciliation among former antagonists. Though one hears occasional talk of recriminations for past wrongs most Kikuyus will jump at the chance to explain how President Kenyatta brought the people together after one of the bloodiest civil conflicts in modern African history.[77]

From the point of view of a Government that wants a cohesive Kikuyu community, the picture looks bleak if one looks at fragmentation and indebtedness. There are modifying factors, however. Land has continued to fragment under population pressures, despite land consolidation and registration. Government's hopes for a small-farmer middle class to arise which would be an element

[77] Stockton, *op.cit.*, p. 3.

of stability in the political and social structure do not appear to have borne fruit. As Leys argues, the basis provided by the consolidation for the emergence of capitalist farming was too narrow to restructure the social and economic system of the area (Central Province).[78] The colonial administration had considered 7.5 acres a minimum economic holding. At the time of land consolidation, 86 percent of all holdings in Central Province were under 7.5 acres.[79] In reality, even what appeared as single holdings were often two or more holdings and existing rights under traditional tenure did not in reality disappear when freehold came about legally. The number of viable holdings among the Kikuyu is small and not all of them are farmed by full-time farmers, the other half being owned by businessmen or professionals who commute to their farms on weekends and/or who have relatives or friends manage farms for them. Sorrenson put the number of economic holdings at 5,000 or 14 percent in 1966 in Kikuyuland.[80] Larger holdings wind up supporting larger numbers of people. In the early 1960s, there were only 2,900 holdings over 15 acres in all of the Kikuyu country. These accounted for less than 10 percent of total holdings and they supported fourteen people per holding on average. A sizable proportion of the larger holdings were really multiple small plots.[81]

Leys argues that in the resettlement areas as well fragmentation of land has been taking place *de facto*.

[78] Leys, "Politics in Kenya," pp. 316-319. The following discussion on land size and fragmentation depends heavily on Leys's excellent work.

[79] *Ibid.*, p. 318. Land consolidation was just about complete in Central Province among both Kikuyu and Embu by 1960.

[80] *Ibid.*, p. 319, citing Sorrenson, *op.cit.*, p. 233.

[81] Leys, "Politics in Kenya," p. 319.

Land is being sold even in the high-density schemes where plots were to be 24 acres. And in places where a settler stays on the original plot, he faces the pressures from landless relatives. Leys and Ruthenberg both see the settlement areas as becoming like the old Kikuyu reserves (the original Kikuyu homeland areas).[82] The characteristics are: absenteeism by heads of household who look for work in the towns; the proliferation of dwelling units on the land, which uses up farming acres; and much land and effort going to food crops for subsistence.

People in leadership roles can be distinguished by size of land holdings from their neighbors but it is not evident that an economically based political class can be marked out. In one densely settled but non-Kikuyu division of Western Province, five of six chiefs in the division had permanent holdings with an average of five acres. This made them moderately well-off compared to their neighbors. It was enough of a distinction with their salaries so that two served as KANU chairmen of the division and ran for Parliament in 1963. Indeed, politics had been the vehicle for their appointment to administrative positions.[83] In Nyeri, leaders and nonleaders were also differ-

---

[82] *Ibid.*, p. 323. Also see Ruthenberg, *op.cit.*, pp. 93-94.

[83] Nicholas Nyangira, "The Role of Chiefs and Sub Chiefs in Administration in Vihiga," IDS Staff Paper No. 68, Nairobi, April 1970. After 1965, district commissioners appointed chiefs. Nyangira reports that there were 63 subchiefs in the division. This was the lowest salaried appointment in the provincial administration as village headmen are not salaried. Of the 63 subchiefs, one-quarter owed their appointments to former members of Parliament. They were rewarded for party services, and they see their appointments as patronage ones even though the district commissioner formally makes the appointment. They get only about 50 pounds per year. One provincial commissioner I

entiated by holdings and agricultural characteristics (see
Table XVI and Table XVII).

TABLE XVI
LAND HOLDINGS OF NYERI LEADERS
AND ALL NYERI PLOTS

Acreage	Leaders (percent)	Nyeri District (percent)
0-4 acres	22.4	60.15
4.1-8 acres	38.4	29.35
8.1-15 acres	25.0	8.77
15.1 or more acres	12.5	1.85

SOURCE: Stockton, *op.cit.*, p. 4.

TABLE XVII
AGRICULTURAL CHARACTERISTICS OF LEADERS
AND NONLEADERS IN NYERI

Characteristic	Leaders (percent)	Nonleaders (percent)
Grows cash crops	81	55
Hires help on farm	59	32
Uses fertilizer or hybrid maize	41	32

SOURCE: Stockton, *op.cit.*, p. 4.

How significant are these differences? It is true that
"better" farmers have access to loans. Most small-holders'

interviewed said that the feeling among chiefs and subchiefs that
they would lose their jobs if they were not on good terms with
local politicians was gradually fading away. He said this, ap-
plauding the trend.

175

loans have been channeled through the Agricultural Finance Corporation (AFC) and Government itself admitted that only a very small fraction would benefit from them. In 1966, the *1966-70 Five Year Plan* anticipated that only 3 percent of Kenya land-owning peasantry (excluding pastoralists) would benefit from AFC loans. The idea was to lend to some 30,000 farmers in 18 districts. But fears of default, scarcity of Government's financial resources, and administrative weaknesses which limited the ability to give loans and agricultural extension assistance meant that only already fairly well-off peasants would benefit from the small-holder loan scheme.[84] There has been diversion of small-farmer loans to larger farmers through local mechanisms too, e.g., control of cooperatives, influence on local boards. Much hope has been placed on cooperatives as mechanisms for upgrading poor farmers. In Kenya, cooperatives have not modified existing economic inequalities.[85]

Vasthoff's study shows that prior to 1966 loans were given to a range of farm sizes. In the Rift Valley, the farms were large by Kenya standards; in a sample of twenty Rift Valley (Nandi) farms, most were 40 acres or more. In Kiambu District, of Central Province, however, while a few large farms showed up in a sample of 28, two-thirds of the farms were under 13 acres. This meant that Kikuyu small holders, but not very small holders, were able to get loans.[86]

[84] Republic of Kenya, *Development Plan, 1966-70* (Nairobi: Government Printer, 1966), p. 133. Loans were also given for specific crops, e.g., tea farmers received loans from the Kenya Tea Development Agency.

[85] Goran Hyden, "Can Cooperatives Make it in Africa?" *Africa Report*, Vol. 15, No. 9 (December 1970), pp. 12-15. Also see Moris, *op.cit.*, p. 407.

[86] Josef Vasthoff, *Small Farm Credit and Development* (Munich: Weltforum Verlag, 1968), pp. 37-40.

Since it was, on the whole, more prosperous farmers who were able to get loans, the extremely heavy indebtedness that showed up in Government figures even before the resettlement-loans schemes was occurring among relatively prosperous farmers.[87] Of course, poorer farmers may well have been undergoing heavy indebtedness through nongovernmental channels. We have already noted that loan defaulting has been extreme among both small and larger farmers on settlement schemes. It became so severe that:

> The emphasis on loan repayment and threat of summary dismissal have combined to produce on the settlement schemes some of the same insecurity that preceded land consolidation in the Kikuyu reserves.[88]

In other words, African farmers in Kenya share indebtedness and they are in the company of the professional middle classes who have borrowed to buy land, build and rent houses, and enter into businesses.[89]

Does fragmentation of land, indebtedness, and differentiation of land holdings mean that stability cannot be maintained in Kenya because an alliance between a Government elite and a rural socioeconomic class cannot be created?[90] To some extent, inequalities of land holdings are modified by short-run adjustments which work to equalize access to agrarian resources. When the larger farmers buy up plots in densely settled areas they usually

[87] *Ibid.*, p. 37 gives figures for indebtedness as of June 30, 1966.

[88] Harbeson, *op.cit.*

[89] Njonjo, *op.cit.*, calls this group "debtors in good standing" as they are heavily mortgaged and dependent on the good will of the state.

[90] For a discussion of this alliance in developing countries see Samuel P. Huntington, *Political Order, passim.*

put a relative on the land.[91] Moreover, as the settlement schemes themselves appear to look more and more like the old Kikuyu reserves, they appear, as Leys puts it, as an extension of peasant society, as a device for dealing with an expanding peasantry through internal migration into the former enclave of capitalist farming.[92] If the base for a rural middle class is too narrow in Kenya, may it not be possible that Kenya is creating a peasant society, at least in its densely settled central areas, without that much differentiation within it except as between a few wealthy farmers and a mass of peasant cultivators? Might Kenya develop a pattern on the land where there are some few capitalist farmers but where, beyond that, economic differentiation is not so significant between everyone else? Tanzania had tried to deliberately slow up the hiring of labor, abolish freehold in land, and create a cooperative base and/or communal based rural society via legislation, political pressure, and leadership exhortation.[93] Might Kenya evolve an equality of small farmers through the workings of population pressure, kinship ties, and market forces where land fragmentation rather than consolidation occurs and stratified classes on the land do not develop?

The only detailed study of income differentiation among Kikuyu peasants is the *Economic Survey of Central Province, 1963-64.* The *Survey* shows that distribution of land and income was within a fairly narrow range. Over three-quarters of all households had incomes under

[91] Moris, *op.cit.*, p. 400.

[92] Leys, "Politics in Kenya," p. 326.

[93] For a discussion of the Tanzania experiment see Julius Nyerere, "Socialism and Rural Development in Nyerere," *Freedom and Socialism* (Nairobi: Oxford University Press, 1968), pp. 337-366. For analysis of this experiment see Bienen, *Tanzania*, pp. 406-447.

$300 a year.[94] While it is true that over 20 percent of the land was in the hands of 7.1 percent of the households and that over 30 percent of the households were farming fewer than 2 acres a plot and that this totaled only 13 percent of total acreage, it is also true that over 70 percent of all households operated in plots no larger than 6 acres.[95] Above all, the average size of a farm for the 4.3 percent of households with the highest annual income (over $700 a year) was not immense: it was only 15.4 acres. The average size of the richest households on the largest plots was larger than the poorest households on the smallest plots—some three times larger in size of household.[96]

Moris states that 15 acres would be a handsome plot in Embu district and 30 acres would be very large indeed.[97] He gives the following figures for landless and average size of holdings.

One has to take these figures with care. To some extent, landless in Kiambu have greater opportunities for employment in Nairobi since they are nearest to the city. And Kiambu has more specialization in cash crops so that landless can be hired in the rural areas. There are several peri-urban villages in Kiambu which inflate the landless figures. Also, it is risky to assume that larger plots are always operated as single farm units. Land is often rented out on the larger plots to clients who are given patches to work for themselves.[98]

Nor is it clear what land differentiation means in terms of life styles. Leys concludes that real discontinuity of

[94] Leys, "Politics in Kenya," p. 328, citing *Economic Survey of Central Province*, p. 31, Table 30.

[95] *Ibid.*, again citing *Economic Survey*.

[96] *Ibid.*   [97] Moris, *op.cit.*, p. 196.

[98] *Ibid.*, p. 199.

TABLE XVIII
LAND HOLDINGS IN CENTRAL PROVINCE

District	Landless (percent)	Average Size of Holdings (acres)
Kiambu	40.9	2.6
Fort Hall (Muran'ga)	18	5.2
Nyeri	19.4	3.3
Embu and Kirinyaga	14.7	4.1
Meru	5.3	4.2

SOURCE: Moris, *op.cit.*, p. 36.

NOTE: The old Central Province included Embu and Meru Districts, which are now in Eastern Province.

life styles occurs only with households with an income above $400 per year and that among the 85 percent with incomes less than this there is an equality of poverty among the masses that produces a homogenous life style.[99] Moris sees subtle gradations among farmers. The better-off may use a different kind of soap, have coffee in the morning before going to the fields, have a primus stove, and maybe a radio. But he sees few wealthy people.[100] Stockton, on the other hand, argues that clear-cut stratifications occur within a limited range of acreages in Nyeri district. While most farms are small and the average has fewer than 4 acres, with only 10 percent above

[99] Leys, "Politics in Kenya," p. 328. Again using the *Economic Survey*, p. 61, Table 72.
[100] Moris, *op.cit.*, p. 199.

8 acres, the difference made by an acre or two is not insignificant.[101] Not only do 6 acres represent 50 percent more land than the average, but the additional 2 acres may represent the marginal difference between the amount of land needed to sustain the family and the amount needed to grow cash crops. A 2-acre stand of well-managed tea can produce crops worth up to $500 per annum, a level attained by fewer than 2 percent of the farms sampled.[102]

It is hard to know what the political consequences of differences of life styles and incomes may be.[103] So far, the evidence is that there has not been a breakdown of rural communities on class grounds and communal solidarities have not been breached as yet. The KPU's appeal to poor farmers did not make much headway in Central Province. Kaggia's appeal to the landless and those with little land did not divide Kikuyu into polarized groups. Factional groups may divide over economic issues but this is not the same thing as positing clear-cut economic classes within Kikuyu society. At this point, political lines do not seem to be drawn between those with a few acres more or less or a hundred dollars a year income more or less. The major basis of differentiation

[101] Stockton, *op.cit.*, p. 4.

[102] *Ibid.*

[103] It has been noted that differences need not be large to create distinctions between overlords and cultivators. If there is sufficient population pressure and scarce land, power differentials appear. See Robert Frykenburg, ed., *Land Control and Social Structure in Indian History* (Madison: University of Wisconsin Press, 1969), esp. pp. 17-31, as cited in John D. Powell, "Stratification, Property, Power and Political Development," paper delivered at the 66th Annual American Political Science Association Meeting, Los Angeles, September 8-12, 1970. Kenya does not yet exhibit this pattern.

in the rural areas is probably not between progressive farmers and less well-off farmers but between those who have a wage employment in the rural sector from Government and those who do not. That is, the division is between civil servants, teachers, the public employees living in rural areas, and those who work on the land. It is really a nonfarm employee vs. farmer or agricultural employee division more than a class division based on land, although it could become transformed if nonfarm wage earners buy land.

Is this division between rural farm and rural nonfarm employees simply a mirror of a rural-urban division in Kenya which should be thought of as the critical class division posited by Fanon for the Third World? If people are differently related to the means of production (farm and nonfarm) and share a consciousness of the political and social consequences of their place in the scheme of production, ought not we to consider this a basic class division? Can a rural-urban division be thought of as the basic cleavage in Kenyan political life?

In the concluding chapter, I argue that rural-urban gaps are bridgeable in Kenya; that the urban sector is not living off an increasingly impoverished rural sector; and that Government has made important inputs into the rural sector which have strengthened its support especially among Kikuyu.

V

Conclusion: Support for the Regime

Kenya is not a society free from severe ethnic and economic tensions. Kenya's ruling institutions do not operate smoothly to deal with the country's problems. Nonetheless, despite the extreme ethnic tensions, despite a faction-ridden political system, the Kenyan regime has maintained a strong base of support.

Population growth cannot be absorbed by the urban sector and it creates tremendous difficulties for Government. The cities cannot accommodate vast numbers of would-be migrants and permanent jobs cannot be found for all those already in the towns. Land consolidation and land resettlement did not solve Kenya's rural problems. They did not end land hunger nor did they create a stable bourgeoisie on the land. But Kenya's peasantry is not becoming increasingly impoverished and pushed off the land.[1] Moris sees an average income for households in Central Kenya of close to $300 if one imputes to farmers the value of production they consume.[2] Peasants have encroached on the former big farm or capitalist farming sector and some better-off farmers have taken advantage of new trade and business opportunities.

If population continues to grow at high rates, Kenya's arable land cannot be encroached on indefinitely. Open-

[1] For an argument about the impoverishment of African peasantries see Giovanni Arrighi and John Saul, "Nationalism and Revolution in Sub-Saharan Africa," in Ralph Miliband and John Saville, eds., *The Socialist Register, 1969* (London: 1969).

[2] Moris, *op.cit.*, p. 408.

ing up new land is costly and capital-consuming because it frequently requires draining or irrigation. Thus the future is hardly one to be sanguine about from the point of view of a regime that is sensitive to and responsive to peasant demands and has real roots and political support in the countryside. But that Government has responded to small and middle-sized farmers cannot be denied.

Government has provided increased schooling and made medical services free; it abolished the Graduated Personal Tax for the lowest income groups, and it taxed the urban rich a bit more; it began to control the price of basic food stuffs and clothing. In the new Five Year Plan, Government states its intention to improve free services, meet needs for improved feeder roads for small farmers, push toward universal and free primary school, and use its funds in the agricultural sphere to improve efficiency and productivity in programs that will involve a high proportion of farmers, whereas its past extension and loans programs have been aimed at a small percentage of farmers, probably around 15 percent of the total.[3] While the Second Five Year Plan does not stress resettlement, it is envisioned that 33,000 unemployed and landless squatters will be settled on low-cost schemes beyond those already resettled.

The Government counts on, and to a large extent receives, a certain realism among the population about what is possible mixed with personal optimism about the future that the survey data indicates many people share. At the same time, survey data does not establish that people immediately expect far-reaching changes.[4]

[3] See L. D. Smith, "Agricultural and Rural Development in Kenya," *East Africa Journal*, Vol. 7, No. 3 (March 1970), and Leys, "Kenya's Second Development Plan," pp. 6-12.

[4] Ross, *op.cit.*, and Hopkins, *op.cit., passim.* Surveys in many

Conclusion

There is, indeed, discontent with farming as a means of earning a livelihood as compared to an urban wage job and people still expect their children to get places in secondary school in much higher proportions than they will be able to achieve. Yet the sights of school-leavers themselves seem to be coming down. Moreover, studies of rural-urban migration in Kenya show a preference among urban migrants to live in previous rural locations if a similar job paying the same wages were available.[5] This is a big "if" in Kenya but it does mean that programs to improve rural life find great response.[6] Aspiring individuals frequently have a preference to become farmers

countries have shown that poor people often express a desire for more security and comfort in a version of their own lives rather than in a change of state. See Anthony and Elizabeth Leeds, "Brazil and the Myth of Urban Reality: Urban Experience, Work, Values, in Squatments of Rio de Janeiro and Lima," mimeograph paper prepared for the Conference on Urbanization and Work in Modernizing Societies, St. Thomas, Virgin Islands, 1967. Also see Anthony Oberschall, "Rising Expectations, National Unity and Political Turmoil," paper presented at the African Studies Association Meetings, New York, November 1967. Oberschall's surveys of Ugandans show that most would like to possess basic items that they do not have but that expectations about acquisitions are realistic. Court and Prewitt, *op.cit.*, p. 10, say about the secondary students they sampled in Kenya, "Not only is there a realistic consensus on the means to personal and national progress but there also appears to be a realistic awareness of where national resources are concentrated, both by those whose regional reference group are getting a disproportionate share of the national cake and by those who are getting a smaller share."

[5] Rempel, Harris, and Todaro, *op.cit.*, pp. 95, 175.

[6] Stockton, *op.cit.*, p. 7, does say that low income is not the only reason for disliking farm life among the Nyeri farmers that he interviewed. Other contributing factors mentioned often were long periods of inactivity, isolation from the excitement

185

but they want to be modern cash crop farmers, not traditional subsistence ones.

Among primary students, farming ranks as the "best" job in all the regions. And it ranks as a "best" job in urban areas as well as rural ones.

However, when primary pupils were asked what job they preferred rather than what was the best job, farming dropped from 29 percent of the "best" category to 7 percent of the "preferred" choices. Only 16 percent of those who had listed farming as the "best" also preferred it as an occupation themselves; still this small group contained 70 percent of all those who preferred farming.[7] I interpret this fall-off as a function of feelings about low income from farming as compared to anticipated income from urban jobs. The question about the "best" job tapped a realistic response. The "best" was in terms of likely possibilities.

Court and Prewitt presented a sample of secondary students with a list of jobs and asked them to indicate on a three point scale their personal preference for doing this

---

of urban life, and the insecurity of crop failures. The last factor is subject to change through new agricultural techniques. The "bright lights" theory of urban migration which emphasizes the social and entertainment attractions of cities has been argued against by John Harris and Michael P. Todaro in "Wage Policy and Employment in a Developing Economy," IDS Staff Paper No. 272, Nairobi, November 1968; also see Michael P. Todaro, "Urban Unemployment in East Africa: An Economic Analysis of Policy Alternatives," *East African Economic Review*, Vol. 4 (1968), pp. 17-36.

[7] Koff, *op.cit.* Also see P. Hoad, "A New Look at Primary School Leavers," University of East Africa Social Science Conference Paper, 1969, found that primary students wanted to be modern farmers.

TABLE XIX

Ten Jobs Most Frequently Chosen as "Best"
by Primary Students

Job	Rural *(percent)*	Urban *(percent)*
1. Cash crop farmer	27	22
2. Primary school teacher	16	17
3. Government Minister	10	3
4. MP	7	4
5. Clerk, secretary	6	9
6. Doctor	6	12
7. Engineer	6	12
8. Nurse	5	3
9. Policeman	3	2
10. Army private	2	1
Percent of Total Choices	88	85
Total Nos.	456	127

SOURCE: David Koff, "Perspectives of Kenya Primary Pupils," in Sheffield, *Education*, pp. 398-401.

job (Table XX). When secondary students were asked to rank the importance of jobs in the development of Kenya, teacher was put first or second in all the provinces sampled and farmer was put second or first.[8]

It is no surprise to learn that Kenyan university students too do not share primary students' attitudes about desired occupations. University students, however, are not going to have to live on the land (Table XXI).

[8] *Ibid.*, Table 8.

187

TABLE XX

RANK-ORDERING OF PERSONAL JOB PREFERENCE, BY PROVINCE
JOBS RANK-ORDERED ON BASIS OF PROPORTION PREFERRING

Province	Assistant Agricultural Officer	Secondary School Teacher	Accounts Clerk in Government Ministry	Garage Mechanic	Farmer with one acre of coffee	Shop Owner
Western	2	1	3	4	5	6
Nyanza	1	2	3	4	5	6
Rift	1	3.5	2	3.5	5	6
Central	1	2	3	4	5	6
East	1	2	3	4.5	4.5	6
Coast	1	2	4	3	5	6

Kendall's Coefficient of Concordance .92

SOURCE: Court and Prewitt, *op.cit.*, p. 9 and TABLE 7.

NOTE: Their questionnaire was administered to 1210 secondary students at a national sample of 23 schools. The exclusion of Nairobi and Northeast Province leaves a sample of 1124 students.

TABLE XXI
DESIRED OCCUPATION AFTER GRADUATION
FROM UNIVERSITY

Job	Kenya (percent)	Tanzania (percent)	Uganda (percent)
Teaching	30	37	32
Civil Service	20	17	21
Medicine	19	8	9
Research	5	9	10
Other professional	11	14	7
Agriculture	5	3	4
Politics	1	1	1
Military	2	4	1
Business	3	3	6
No answer, or don't know	4	4	9
	N=205	N=479	N=550

SOURCE: Joel Barkan, "African University Students: Presumptive Elite or Upper-Middle Class," in Prewitt, *op.cit.*, p. 184. Barkan's survey was carried out in 1966 and 1967. The Kenyan students he surveyed were studying at Makerere University College, Kampala and University College, Dar es Salaam.

The Kenya Government has been responsive to the necessity of a farming existence for the great majority of Kenyans. The claim has been made that Kenya has the most extensive measures for rural growth in Africa.[9] Certainly, the development of agriculture in Central Province and parts of the Rift Valley is a remarkable achievement

[9] Jon Moris, "An Appraisal of Rural Development in Kenya," unpublished paper, Nairobi, 1969.

considering the dualism of the rural economy and the low standards in the peasant sector which prevailed in Kenya. "So far in Africa, none of the alternative approaches, whether more socialistic or more capitalistic, have demonstrated equal results on this large a scale."[10] While it is by no means certain that the Kenya Government will succeed in maintaining rural support among its critical constituencies, its policies have been aimed at doing this from the inception of the regime.

The safety valves of Africanization and land settlement have operated so far. Most observers are agreed that there has been a good deal of social mobility from one generation to the next and that parental wealth has not been critical so far in individual attainment of elite status.[11] There is, however, a strong correlation between income and education in the rural and urban areas. A recent study showed marked differences in income accruing to educational differences when figures were adjusted for acreage and family size.[12] The question is

[10] Moris, "The Agrarian Revolution," p. 13.

[11] Koff and Von Der Muhll's study of secondary students shows that few of the sample have parents who attain the same level of education. The parents were generally peasant farmers with at most a few years of primary education. They conclude that parental wealth was not critical for the 3 percent who made it to secondary school. Koff and Von Der Muhll, *op.cit.*, p. 84.

[12] A study by Heinrich Thias with Martin Carnoy as consultant was prepared for the World Bank and titled *Cost Benefit Analysis in Education in Kenya*, International Bank for Reconstruction and Development, No. EV 173, Washington, November 1969. This study was referred to by Prewitt, *op.cit.* It stated that in a 30-40 age group, where the head of household was literate, average earnings were about $112 compared to $70 for illiterate heads of household. Where the head of household had 1-3 years of schooling, average earnings were $300, increasing to $410 with 9 or more years. Performance on examinations was correlated

whether people of high education will be able in the future to pass on opportunities for education and thus wealth to their children. At this point, it is too soon to talk about a class defined by wealth which can perpetuate itself in Kenya. But it is also true that we must be careful about extrapolating past mobility trends into the future. There is likely to be a slowdown of the rate of growth of the African elite relative to the African population as a whole compared to the 1950s and 1960s. There are already attempts on the part of people in the trading and business groups to limit access to the African elite by creating trade and business monopolies.[13] Nor is it likely that university spaces will be increased rapidly.

In the Kenyan social and economic context, KANU has been an arena where elites can compete, where some social mobility is possible through its organizations and through which local favors can be carried out. The regime has not tried to construct a party that reaches out for all members of the body politic and brings them under its control. It has not tried to forge an organizational weapon to change the normative and social structure of society. Quite the contrary, it has relied on existing social

---

with earnings too. Whereas Von Der Muhll and Koff tended to downplay the relationship between parents' education and students' education, the Thias study argued that if the parents were literate, respondents in their sample had a 60 percent higher education than those respondents whose parents were not educated.

[13] For an analysis of attempts by Africans to restrict access to trade and business see Colin Leys, "The Limits of Capitalism: The Formation of the Monopolistic Petty Bourgeoisie in Kenya," unpublished paper, 1972. Leys sees in Kenya the creation of what he calls a monopolistic petty bourgeoisie dependent on the state for maintaining its privileged position.

and ethnic formations to carry out rural and urban development.

The Civil Service in Kenya provides services and controls political participation; it does not mobilize large numbers of people or persuade them through exhortation and appeals to ideologically formulated goals. I have argued that this is not necessary in Kenya. I have also argued that Government, through the provincial administration, is responsive to grass-roots demands. Patron-client networks continue to provide mobility for some individuals and to fill gaps between ethnic groups and rural and urban dwellers. They cut across regionalisms, tribalisms, class and institutional networks as high-level leaders recruit followers and make alliances of an extremely heterogeneous nature. This does not mean that the loose and fluid personal networks create national unity by fostering supra-tribal cooperation or by creating permanent loyalties beyond the regional, tribal, or institutional units. Members of patron-client networks who are low down on the ladder are usually in contact with people like themselves. Furthermore, attachments are often transitory. Nonetheless, if we focus only on political units defined by class, ethnic, or institutional criteria, we shall miss much of the group context of Kenyan political life.

The Kenyans who think that "a man who works hard enough can improve his life, even if Government does not make conditions better"[14] may be optimistic. But if a poor farmer does take action, he is more likely to enter

[14] Koff and Von Der Muhll, *op.cit.*, p. 87, note that 80 percent of the Kenyan primary students and 71 percent of the secondary students sampled agreed with an ethic of self-improvement compared to 73 percent of the Tanzanian primary students and 63 percent of the Tanzanian secondary students in their sample.

into a client relationship with one of the better-off members of the community than to challenge the ongoing system.[15] For the individual challenge has high risks. The political and Civil Service elite skims the cream off the top in Kenya. Nonetheless, the mode of local political machines, patron-client networks, and personal decision-making at the top with decisions implemented through the Civil Service corresponds to reality. That "reality" includes strong ethnic identification, the maintenance of rural-urban ties among migrants, and weak class consciousness where the relatively underprivileged hope to ascend in the social and economic hierarchy through individual and ethnic movement rather than through class action.

Leaders can act without effective restraints on them. That is, neither constitutional provisions nor interest groups nor the electoral system can check governmental leaders' executive powers in the short run. But this does not mean that broad functional interests are not represented in politics. They are in Kenya. There is a great deal of localized determination of political life on local issues. For all the strength of executive authority when wielded against specific targets at a given point in time, power remains dispersed in Kenya and social control from the center is not all encompassing. Large numbers of people get what they want from politics in Kenya. For many peasant farmers what they want is to be left alone politically and to be provided with agricultural services and schooling opportunities for children. Political participation for them takes place at local levels and linkage to the center is accomplished by the flow of services to rural areas. For elites, political participation is essentially the competition for positions, status, and wealth in a host

[15] Hyden, *op.cit.*, p. 14.

of district and national arenas. This competition has remained fluid if not completely open. No ethnic groups have been completely frozen out of the system at either the elite or non-elite levels. Relatively good economic performance allows for increasing opportunities among elites and for the continued flow of services to rural areas. It does not guarantee that political leaders will remain sensitive to rural demands but it makes it easier for them to accommodate demands.

A. PARTICIPATION AND SUPPORT

There is no reason to expect a crisis in Kenya resulting from weak institutions unable to accommodate demands and stressed by political participation. Not all increases in political participation lead to increased economic and social demands. A population that feels it can participate in local politics and can have a say about national representation may moderate demands. And, when services are provided to the rural population, and certain demands are met, participation may be circumscribed without creating a crisis situation. Demands and participation must be kept analytically separate. Increased participation need not lead to increased effective demands. There are tradeoffs between participation and the satisfaction of social and economic demands that have been apparent in Kenya. And leaders have received good information both at the center and in the rural areas by not closing off participation.

The model that has been put forward of increased participation from below leading to a rise in effective demands which in turn stress weak institutions in developing countries needs revision.[16] Political participation

[16] Huntington, *Political Order in Changing Societies, passim.*

takes place in different contexts, national and local, and it has different forms and meanings for different groups. Political participation may not stress national institutions if major arenas of politics are local ones. Political participation can also be reined in at various points without necessarily a regime becoming unresponsive to its population.

We have perhaps become so conscious of the weakness of regimes in Africa and the inability of central governments to deal with the problems of their societies that we have not explored enough the sources of regime support. The limited sphere of governing has been stressed rather than the contacts between regime and population.[17]

Of course, it can be argued that Kenya is an atypical African country. It does not exhibit patterns of coup and counter-coup which characterize a number of African states and it is relatively well endowed. All the more reason to examine Kenyan patterns of participation and control. Furthermore, Kenya does provide an example of an African regime that retains support among important elements of its society in the context of political stability and comparatively high rate of economic growth but which also has extreme ethnic tensions, population pressures, a fragmented ruling party. Kenya's institutions are not strong unless we measure them *ex post facto* by the success of the regime, which is no independent measure at all. And Kenya continues to have more political participation both at local and national levels and among elites and non-elites alike than most African states. This suggests that perhaps it makes no sense to look at ratios of institutionalization and participation without emphasizing the content of policies formulated at the center and the way they are received throughout the country. The

[17] Zolberg, *Creating Political Order.*

nature of participation, its forms, arenas, targets, and the kinds of demands that are put forward must be made very explicit if the nature of regime support or instability is to be made clear. This recognition forces us, of course, to look at the specifics of politics in a given country and warns us against applying formulas before they are operationalized enough to take account of these specifics.

Selected Bibliography

BOOKS

Almond, Gabriel, and Verba, Sidney. *The Civic Culture.* Boston: Little, Brown, 1963.

Apter, David. *Ghana in Transition.* New York: Atheneum, 1963.

―――. *The Politics of Modernization.* Chicago: The University of Chicago Press, 1965.

Barnett, Donald L., and Njama, Karari. *Mau Mau From Within.* London: MacGibbon and Kee, 1966.

Bennett, George, and Rosberg, Carl G. *The Kenyatta Election: Kenya 1960-61.* London: Oxford University Press, 1961.

Bienen, Henry. *Tanzania: Party Transformation and Economic Development.* Princeton: Princeton University Press, 1970.

Blundell, Michael. *So Rough A Wind.* London: Weidenfeld and Nicolson, 1964.

Carey-Jones, N. S. *The Anatomy of Uhuru: Dynamics and Problems of African Independence in an Age of Conflict.* New York: Frederick Praeger, 1966.

Chambers, Robert. *Settlement Schemes in Tropical Africa.* New York: Frederick Praeger, 1969.

Cowan, L. Gray. *The Costs of Learning: The Politics of Primary Education in Kenya.* New York: Teachers College Press, 1970.

de Wilde, John C. *Experience With Agricultural Development in Tropical Africa*, Vol. 2. Baltimore: Johns Hopkins Press, 1967.

Diamond, Stanley, and Burke, Fred, eds. *The Transformation of East Africa.* New York: Basic Books, 1964.

Djilas, Milovan. *The New Class.* Frederick Praeger, 1957.

Fanon, Frantz. *The Wretched of the Earth.* New York: Grove Press, 1963.

Foster, Philip, and Zolberg, Aristide, eds. *Ghana and the Ivory Coast.* Chicago and London: The University of Chicago Press, 1971.

Gertzel, Cherry. *The Politics of Independent Kenya.* Nairobi: East African Publishing House, 1970.

————, Goldschmidt, Maure, and Rothchild, Donald, eds. *Government and Politics in Kenya.* Nairobi: East African Publishing House, 1969.

Ghai, D., and McAuslan, J.P.W.B. *Public Law and Political Change in Kenya.* London: Oxford University Press, 1970.

Hopkins, Nicholas S. *Popular Government in an African Town.* Chicago: University of Chicago Press, 1972.

Huntington, Samuel P. *Political Order in Changing Societies.* New Haven: Yale University Press, 1968.

Hyden, Goran, Jackson, Robert, and Okumu, John, eds. *Development Administration: The Kenyan Experience.* Nairobi: Oxford University Press, 1970.

Itote, Waruhiu. *"Mau Mau" General.* Nairobi: East African Publishing House, 1967.

Kenyatta, Jomo. *Facing Mt. Kenya.* London: Mercury Books, 1961.

————. *Suffering Without Bitterness.* Nairobi: East African Publishing House, 1968.

Kilson, Martin. *Political Change in a West African State: A Study of the Modernization Process in Sierra Leone.* Cambridge: Harvard University Press, 1966.

Lee, J. M. *African Armies and Civil Order.* London: Chatto and Windus, 1969.

Marris, Peter, and Somerset, Anthony. *African Businessmen.* London: Routledge and Kegan Paul, 1969.

Melson, Robert, and Wolpe, Howard, eds. *Nigeria: Modernization and the Politics of Communalism.* East Lansing: Michigan State University Press, 1971.

Milbrath, Lester. *Political Participation.* Chicago: Rand McNally, 1962.

Odinga, Oginga. *Not Yet Uhuru.* New York: Hill and Wang, 1967.

Ominde, S. H. *Land and Population Movements of Kenya.* Evanston: Northwestern University Press, 1968.

Oser, Jacob. *Promoting Economic Development: With Illustrations From Kenya.* Nairobi: East African Publishing House. 1967.

Prewitt, Kenneth, ed. *Education and Political Values: An East African Case Study.* Nairobi: East African Publishing House, 1971.

Pye, Lucian, and Verba, Sidney, eds. *Political Culture and Political Development.* Princeton: Princeton University Press, 1965.

Rosberg, Carl G., and Nottingham, John. *The Myth of Mau Mau.* New York: Frederick Praeger, 1966.

Ruthenberg, Hans. *African Agricultural Production: Development Policy in Kenya, 1952-1965.* Berlin: Springer-Verlag, 1966.

Sheffield, James, ed. *Education, Employment and Rural Development.* Nairobi: East African Publishing House, 1967.

Sklar, Richard. *Nigerian Political Parties.* Princeton University Press, 1963.

Soja, Edward. *The Geography of Modernization in Kenya.* Syracuse: Syracuse University Press, 1968.

Sorrenson, M.P.K. *Land Reform in the Kikuyu Country.* London: Oxford University Press, 1967.

Townsend, James. *Political Participation in Communist China.* Berkeley: University of California Press, 1967.

Vasthoff, Josef. *Small Farm Credit and Development.* Munich: Weltform Verlag, 1968.

Weiss, Herbert. *Political Protest in the Congo.* Princeton: Princeton University Press, 1967.

Young, Crawford. *Politics in the Congo.* Princeton: Princeton University Press, 1965.

Zolberg, Aristide. *Creating Political Order: The Party-States of West Africa.* Chicago: Rand McNally, 1966.

ARTICLES

Anber, Paul. "Nigeria and the Ibos." *Journal of Modern African Studies.* Vol. 5, No. 2 (September 1967), pp. 163-180.

Arrighi, Giovanni, and Saul, John. "Nationalism and Revolution in Sub-Saharan Africa," in Miliband, Ralph, and Saville, John, eds. *The Socialist Register, 1969.* London: 1969.

Barber, William J. "Land Reform and Economic Change Among African Farmers in Kenya." *Economic Development and Cultural Change,* Vol. 14, No. 1 (October 1970), pp. 6-24.

Barkan, Joel D. "What Makes East African Students Run," *Transition* (Kampala), Vol. 7, No. 37 (1968).

Bennett, George. "Kenya's Little General Election," *World Today,* Vol. 22, No. 8 (August 1966), pp. 336-343.

———. "Opposition in Kenya," in *Opposition in the New African States,* Institute of Commonwealth Studies, University of London, No. 4 (October 1967-March 1968), pp. 55-64.

Bienen, Henry. "The Background," in Bienen, Henry, ed.

The Military and Modernization. Chicago: Atherton-Aldine, 1971, pp. 1-33.

————. "One-Party Systems in Africa," in Huntington, Samuel P. and Moore, Clement, eds. *Authoritarian Politics in Modern Societies.* New York: Basic Books, 1970, pp. 99-127.

————. "Public Order and the Military in Africa: Mutinies in Kenya, Uganda and Tanganyika," in Bienen, Henry, ed. *The Military Intervenes: Case Studies in Political Development.* New York: Russell Sage Foundation, 1968, pp. 35-70.

Bowring, W.J.W. "Competitive Politics in East African Local Government," *The Journal of Developing Areas,* Vol. 5 (October 1970), pp. 43-60.

Deutsch, Karl. "Social Mobilization and Political Development," *American Political Science Review,* Vol. 55, No. 3 (September 1961), pp. 493-514.

Eckstein, Harry. "A Perspective on Comparative Politics, Past and Present," in Eckstein, Harry and Apter, David, eds. *Comparative Politics: A Reader.* New York: The Free Press, 1963.

Gertzel, Cherry. "The Provincial Administration in Kenya," *Journal of Commonwealth Political Studies,* Vol. 4, No. 3 (November 1966), pp. 201-215.

Ghai, Dharam. "Employment Performance, Prospects and Policies in Kenya," *East Africa Journal,* Vol. 7, No. 11 (November 1970), pp. 4-11.

Gluckman, Max. "Tribalism in Modern British Central Africa," *Cahiers d'Etudes Africaines,* Vol. 1, No. 3 (1960), pp. 55-70.

Good, Kenneth. "Kenyatta and the Organization of KANU," *Canadian Journal of African Studies,* Vol. 11, No. 2 (1968).

Green, Reginald. "Four African Development Plans: Ghana, Kenya, Nigeria, and Tanzania," *Journal of Modern African Studies*, Vol. 3, No. 2 (1965), pp. 253-274.

Harbeson, John. "Land Reform and Politics in Kenya," *Journal of Modern African Studies*, Vol. 9, No. 2 (August 1971), pp. 231-252.

Hunter, Guy. "Development Administration in East Africa," *Journal of Administration Overseas*, Vol. 6, No. 1 (January 1967).

Huntington, Samuel P. "Political Development and Political Decay," *World Politics*, Vol. 17, No. 3 (1965), pp. 386-430.

Hyden, Goran. "Can Cooperatives Make it in Africa?" *Africa Report*, Vol. 15, No. 9 (December 1970), pp. 12-15.

Hyden, Goran. "Local Government Reform in Kenya," *East Africa Journal*, Vol. 7, No. 4 (April 1970), pp. 19-24.

Koff, David. "Kenya's Little General Election," *Africa Report*, Vol. 11, No. 7 (October 1966), pp. 57-60.

Lemarchand, Rene, and Legg, Keith. "Political Clientelism and Development: A Preliminary Analysis," *Comparative Politics*, Vol. 4, No. 2 (January 1972), pp. 149-178.

Leys, Colin. "Politics in Kenya: The Development of Peasant Society," *British Journal of Political Science*, Vol. 1, No. 3 (1971), pp. 307-337.

———. "Kenya's Second Development Plan," *East Africa Journal*, Vol. 7, No. 3 (March 1970), pp. 6-12.

Marris, Peter. "The Social Barriers to African Entrepreneurship," *Journal of Development Studies*, Vol. 15, No. 1 (October 1968), pp. 29-39.

Bibliography

Meisler, Stanley. "Tribal Politics Harass Kenya," *Foreign Affairs*, Vol. 49, No. 1 (October 1970), pp. 111-121.

Mitchell, Frank. "Macro-Aspects of the Plan," *East Africa Journal*, Vol. 7, No. 3 (March 1970).

Mohiddin, Ahmed. "Sessional Paper No. 10 Revisited," *East Africa Journal*, Vol. 6, No. 3 (March 1969), pp. 7-16.

Murray, John. "Succession Prospects in Kenya," *Africa Report*, Vol. 13, No. 8 (November 1968), pp. 44-48.

Nellis, John. "The Administration of Rural Development in Kenya," *East Africa Journal*, Vol. 9, No. 3 (March 1972).

————. "Is the Kenyan Bureaucracy Developmental?" *African Studies Review*, Vol. 14, No. 3 (December 1971), pp. 389-402.

Nelson, Joan. "The Urban Poor: Disruption or Political Integration in Third World Cities," *World Politics*, Vol. 22 (April 1970), pp. 393-414.

O'Connell, James O. "The Inevitability of Instability," *Journal of Modern African Studies*, Vol. 5, No. 2 (September 1967), pp. 181-192.

Okumu, John. "The By-Election in Gem," *East Africa Journal*, Vol. 6, No. 8 (June 1969), pp. 9-17.

————. "Charisma and Politics in Kenya," *East Africa Journal*, Vol. 5, No. 2 (February 1968), pp. 9-16.

Oyugi, W. O. "The Ndhiwa By-Election," *East Africa Journal*, Vol. 7, No. 10 (October 1970), pp. 4-11.

Powell, John Duncan. "Peasant Society and Clientelist Politics," *American Political Science Review*, Vol. 64, No. 2 (June 1970), pp. 411-425.

Rado, Emil. "Employment, Incomes Policy: Kenya's New Development Plan," *East Africa Journal*, Vol. 18, No. 3 (March 1970).

Roth, Gruenther. "Personal Rulership, Patrimonialism

and Empire-building in the New States," *World Politics*, Vol. 20, No. 2 (January 1968), pp. 194-206.

Rothchild, Donald. "Ethnic Inequalities in Kenya," *The Journal of Modern African Studies*, Vol. 7, No. 4 (1969), pp. 689-711.

—————. "Kenya's Africanization Program: Priorities of Development and Equity," *American Political Science Review*, Vol. 64, No. 3 (September 1970), pp. 737-753.

—————. "Kenya's Minorities and the African Crises over Citizenship," *Race*, Vol. 9, No. 4 (1968), pp. 421-437.

Sandbrook, Richard. "Patrons, Clients, and Factions: New Dimensions of Conflict Analysis in Africa," *Canadian Journal of Political Science*, Vol. 5, No. 1 (March 1972), pp. 104-119.

—————. "Patrons, Clients and Unions: The Labour Movement and Political Conflict in Kenya," *Journal of Commonwealth Political Studies*, Vol. 9 (March 1972), pp. 13-27.

Sanger, Clyde, and Nottingham, John. "The Kenya General Election of 1963," *Journal of Modern African Studies*, Vol. 2, No. 1 (1964), pp. 1-40.

Scott, James C. "Corruption, Machine Politics, and Political Change," *American Political Science Review*, Vol. 63, No. 4 (December 1969), pp. 1142-1158.

Segal, Aaron. "The Politics of Land in East Africa," *Africa Report*, Vol. 12, No. 4 (April 1967), pp. 49-50.

Seidman, A. W. "The Agricultural Revolution," *East Africa Journal*, Vol. 7, No. 8 (August 1970), pp. 21-35.

—————. "Comparative Development Strategies in East Africa," *East Africa Journal*, Vol. 7, No. 4 (April 1970), pp. 13-18.

————. "Comparative Industrial Strategies in East Africa," *East Africa Journal*, Vol. 7, No. 6 (June 1970), pp. 18-42.

————. "The Dual Economies of East Africa," *East Africa Journal*, Vol. 7, No. 5 (May 1970), pp. 6-19.

Sklar, Richard. "Political Science and National Integration," *Journal of Modern African Studies*, Vol. 5, No. 1 (May 1967), pp. 1-12.

Smith, L. D. "Agricultural and Rural Development in Kenya, *East Africa Journal*, Vol. 7, No. 3 (March 1970), pp. 46-49.

Stren, Richard. "Factional Politics and Central Control in Mombasa, 1960-1969," *Canadian Journal of African Studies* (Winter 1970), pp. 33-56.

Todaro, Michael P. "Urban Unemployment in East Africa: An Economic Analysis of Policy Alternatives," *East African Economic Review*, Vol. 4 (1968), pp. 17-36.

Towet, Taita. "KANU: The Neglected Constitution," *Kenya Weekly News*. Nakuru: April 18, 1969.

Wallerstein, Immanuel. "Ethnicity and National Integration in West Africa," *Cahiers d'Etudes Africaines*, Vol. 1, No. 3 (1960), pp. 129-139.

Weingrod, Alex. "Patrons, Patronage, and Political Parties," *Comparative Studies in Society and History*, Vol. 10 (July 1968), pp. 377-400.

Whetham, Edith. "Land Reform and Resettlement in Kenya," *East African Journal of Rural Development*, Vol. 1, No. 1 (January 1968), pp. 18-29.

Zolberg, Aristide. "The Structure of Political Conflict in the New States of Tropical Africa," *American Political Science Review*, Vol. 62, No. 1 (March 1968), pp. 70-87.

PAMPHLETS AND MONOGRAPHS

Chaput, Michael, and Venys, Ladislav. *A Survey of the Kenya Elite.* Maxwell Graduate School of Citizenship and Public Affairs, Program of Eastern African Studies, Occasional Paper No. 25. Syracuse University.

Herz, Barbara. *Land Reform in Kenya.* Agency for International Development, Spring Review Country Paper, Washington, June 1970.

KANU *Constitutions.* Various versions, mimeographs.

KANU. *Minutes of the Mombasa Meetings, 1968,* mimeograph.

Nellis, John. *Who Pays Taxes in Kenya?* Research report No. 11. Scandinavian Institute of African Studies, Uppsala, 1972.

Nelson, Joan. *Migrants, Urban Poverty and Instability in Developing Nations.* Harvard University Center of International Affairs, Occasional Paper, Vol. 22 (1968).

Safier, Michael, ed. *The Role of Urban and Regional Planning in National Development in East Africa.* Kampala, The Milton Obote Foundation, 1970.

Sheffield, James. *Education in the Republic of Kenya.* Department of Health, Education and Welfare, Washington, 1971.

The Report of the Select Committee to Investigate Into Possibilities of Africanization in All Fields (with Minutes), mimeograph, Nairobi, 1969.

Verba, Sidney, Nie, Norman, and Kim, Jae-on. *The Modes of Democratic Participation: A Cross National Comparison.* A Sage Professional Paper, Series No. 01-013, Vol. 2, Beverly Hills, 1971.

Bibliography

Wananchi Declaration: The Programme of the Kenya People's Union, Nairobi, n.d.

Weeks, Sheldon. *Divergence in Educational Development: The Case of Kenya and Uganda*. New York: Teachers College Press, 1967.

GOVERNMENT OF KENYA PUBLICATIONS

Economic Survey, 1967. Nairobi: Government Printer, 1968.

Economic Survey, 1969. Nairobi: Government Printer, 1969.

Economic Survey, 1970. Nairobi: Government Printer, 1971.

Economic Survey of Central Province, 1963-64. Nairobi: Statistics Division of Ministry of Economic Planning and Development, 1968.

Kenya Development Plan, 1966-70 Nairobi: Government Printer, 1966.

Kenya Development Plan, 1970-74. Nairobi: Government Printer, 1969.

Kenya Education Commission Report. Nairobi: Government Printer, 1965.

Kenya Population Census, 1969. Nairobi: Government Printer, 1970.

Report of the Commission on Inquiry, 1970-71. Public Service Structure and Remuneration Commission. Nairobi: Government Printer, 1971.

Statistical Abstract, 1965. Nairobi: Statistics Division, Ministry of Economic Development and Planning, 1966.

Statistical Abstract, 1970. Nairobi: Statistics Division, Ministry of Finance and Economic Planning, 1971.

Bibliography

Unpublished Works

Adelman, Irma, and Morris, Cynthia Taft. "A Conceptualization and Analysis of Political Participation in Underdeveloped Countries," Part II, Final Report. Agency for International Development, Washington, February 1971.

Anderson, John. "Education for Self-Reliance." Discussion Paper No. 67. Institute for Development Studies, Nairobi, September 1968.

Bienen, Henry. "The Military and Society in East Africa." Paper presented to the Conference on African Armies, Georgetown University, Center for Strategic Studies, Washington, May 1970.

Bucknall, J. J. "The Role of State Trading in Kenya with Special Reference to the Kenya National Trading Corporation." Staff Paper No. 49, Institute for Development Studies, Nairobi, October 1969.

Court, David, and Prewitt, Kenneth. "Nation Versus Region: Social Learning in Kenyan Secondary Schools." Institute for Development Studies, Nairobi, September 1972.

Diejomah, V. P. "Tax Mobilization and Government Development Financing in Kenya." Staff Paper No. 45, Institute for Development Studies, Nairobi, September 1969.

————. "Financing Local Government Authorities in Kenya." Discussion Paper No. 96, Institute for Development Studies, Nairobi, September 1970.

Hakes, Jay E. "Patronage and Politics in Kenya: A Study of Backbencher Membership on Statutory Boards."

————. "The Parliamentary Party in Kenya." Paper presented at the International Studies Association, South-Southwest Regional Meeting, October 1970.

————. "The Recruitment of Political Leaders in the National Assembly of Kenya," 1970.

————. "The Weakness of Parliamentary Institutions as a Prelude to Military Coups in Africa." Paper presented at the 43d Annual Meeting of the Southern Political Science Association, Gatlinburg, November 1971.

Harbeson, John. "The Kenya Little General Election: A Study in the Problems of Urban Political Integration." Discussion Paper No. 54, Institute for Development Studies, Nairobi, June 1967.

Harris, John, and Todaro, Michael P. "Wage Policy and Employment in a Developing Economy." Staff Paper No. 272, Institute for Development Studies, Nairobi, November 1968.

Heyer, Judith; Ireri, Dunstan; Moris, Jon. "Rural Development in Kenya." Institute for Development Studies, Nairobi 1969.

Hopkins, Raymond. "The Kenyan Legislature: Political Functions and Citizen Perceptions." Shambaugh Conference on Legislative Systems in Developing Countries, University of Iowa, Iowa City, November 1971.

————. "Code Book for the Kenyan Study of Social Mobilization and Political Participation," 1971.

Johnson, George E. "Notes on Wages, Employment and Income Distribution." Institute for Development Studies, Nairobi, 1971.

Kaggia, Bildad. "Autobiography." Nairobi, 1969.

Lamb, Geoffrey. "Politics and Administration in Muran'ga District Kenya." University of Sussex, 1968.

Leys, Colin. "The Limits of Capitalism: The Formation of the Monopolistic Petty Bourgeoisie in Kenya." 1972.

————, and Hyden, Goran. "Elections and Politics in

Single-Party Systems: The Case of Kenya and Tanzania." Nairobi, 1970.

Mitchell, Frank, and Bienen, Henry. "The Study of Efficiency and Organization of Distribution." Staff Paper No. 38, Institute for Development Studies, Nairobi, February 1969.

Moris, Jon. "The Agrarian Revolution in Central Kenya: A Study of Farm Innovation in Embu District." Dissertation presented to Department of Anthropology, Northwestern University, 1970.

————. "An Appraisal of Rural Development in Kenya." Nairobi, 1969.

Mueller, Susanne. "Political Parties in Kenya: Politics of Opposition and Dissent, 1919-1969." Dissertation presented to the Department of Politics, Princeton University, 1972.

Mukuria, W. B. "Harambee Secondary Schools—An Aspect of Self-Help Projects in Kikuyu Division, Kenya." The University of East Africa, University Examinations, Dar-es-Salaam, 1969.

Nathan, Andrew. "Factionalism in Early Republican China: The Politics of the Peking Government, 1918-1920." Dissertation presented to the Department of Government, Harvard University, 1970.

Nguyo, Wilson. "Some Socio-Economic Aspects of Land Settlement in Kenya." Makerere Institute of Social Research Conference Paper, Kampala, January 1967.

Njonjo, Appolo. "Kenya: The Problems of Succession and the Issues Behind the Plot." Princeton, 1971.

Nyangira, Nicholas. "Chiefs' Barazas as Agents of Administration and Political Change." Staff Paper No. 80, Institute for Development Studies, Nairobi, July 1970.

————. "The Role of Chiefs and Sub Chiefs in Administration in Vihiga." Staff Paper No. 68, Institute for Development Studies. Nairobi, April 1970.

Okelo, Jasper. "Know-How and Success in Retail Trade —A Case Study of Traders in River Road." Staff Paper No. 69, Institute for Development Studies, Nairobi, April 1970.

Okumu, John. "The Problems of Party Leadership in Kenya," University of East Africa, Social Science Conference, January 1968.

Powell, John D. "Stratification, Property, Power and Political Development." Paper delivered at the 66th Annual American Political Science Association Meeting, Los Angeles, September 1970.

Prewitt, Kenneth. "Schooling, Stratification and Equality: Notes for Research," Institute for Development Studies, Nairobi, n.d.

Rempel, Henry; Harris, John; Todaro, Michael P. "Rural to Urban Labour Migration: A Tabulation of Responses to the Questionnaire Used in the Migration Survey." Staff Paper No. 39, Institute for Development Studies, Nairobi, March 1970.

Ross, Marc Howard. "Grassroots in the City: Political Participation and Alienation in Nairobi After Independence," Bryn Mawr, 1971.

———. "Urbanization and Political Participation: The Effect of Increasing Scale in Nairobi." Paper presented to the Annual Meeting of the African Studies Association, Boston, October 1970.

Sandberg, Auden. "Generation Conflict and Entrepreneurship in Meru." Staff Paper No. 52, Institute for Development Studies, Nairobi, December 1969.

Stockton, Ronald. "Aspects of Leadership in Nyeri." Staff Paper No. 107, Institute for Development Studies, Nairobi, n.d.

Stren, Richard. "Local Government in Kenya: The Limits of Development Planning." Paper prepared for delivery at the Annual Meeting of the African Studies Association, Montreal, October 1969.

Valentine, Malcom. "Continuity and Change in Luo Social Organization." Kampala, 1965.

Weisner, Thomas. "Studying Rural-Urban Ties: A. Matched Network Sample from Kenya." Forthcoming in O'Barr, Spain, and Tessler, eds., *Solving Problems of Survey Research in Africa.*

Index

213

214

BOOKS WRITTEN
UNDER THE AUSPICES OF THE
CENTER OF INTERNATIONAL STUDIES
PRINCETON UNIVERSITY

Gabriel A. Almond, *The Appeals of Communism* (Princeton University Press 1954)

William W. Kaufmann, ed., *Military Policy and National Security* (Princeton University Press 1956)

Klaus Knorr, *The War Potential of Nations* (Princeton University Press 1956)

Lucian W. Pye, *Guerrilla Communism in Malaya* (Princeton University Press 1956)

Charles De Visscher, *Theory and Reality in Public International Law*, trans. by P. E. Corbett (Princeton University Press 1957; rev. ed. 1968)

Bernard C. Cohen, *The Political Process and Foreign Policy: The Making of the Japanese Peace Settlement* (Princeton University Press 1957)

Myron Weiner, *Party Politics in India: The Development of a Multi-Party System* (Princeton University Press 1957)

Percy E. Corbett, *Law in Diplomacy* (Princeton University Press 1959)

Rolf Sannwald and Jacques Stohler, *Economic Integration: Theoretical Assumptions and Consequences of European Unification*, trans. by Herman Karreman (Princeton University Press 1959)

Klaus Knorr, ed., *NATO and American Security* (Princeton University Press 1959)

Gabriel A. Almond and James S. Coleman, eds., *The Politics of the Developing Areas* (Princeton University Press 1960)

Herman Kahn, *On Thermonuclear War* (Princeton University Press 1960)

Sidney Verba, *Small Groups and Political Behavior: A Study of Leadership* (Princeton University Press 1961)

Robert J. C. Butow, *Tojo and the Coming of the War* (Princeton University Press 1961)

Glenn H. Snyder, *Deterrence and Defense: Toward a Theory of National Security* (Princeton University Press 1961)

Klaus Knorr and Sidney Verba, eds., *The International System: Theoretical Essays* (Princeton University Press 1961)

Peter Paret and John W. Shy, *Guerrillas in the 1960's* (Praeger 1962)

George Modelski, *A Theory of Foreign Policy* (Praeger 1962)

Klaus Knorr and Thornton Read, eds., *Limited Strategic War* (Praeger 1963)

Frederick S. Dunn, *Peace-Making and the Settlement with Japan* (Princeton University Press 1963)

Arthur L. Burns and Nina Heathcote, *Peace-Keeping by United Nations Forces* (Praeger 1963)

Richard A. Falk, *Law, Morality, and War in the Contemporary World* (Praeger 1963)

James N. Rosenau, *National Leadership and Foreign Policy: A Case Study in the Mobilization of Public Support* (Princeton University Press 1963)

Gabriel A. Almond and Sidney Verba, *The Civic Culture: Political Attitudes and Democracy in Five Nations* (Princeton University Press 1963)

Bernard C. Cohen, *The Press and Foreign Policy* (Princeton University Press 1963)

Richard L. Sklar, *Nigerian Political Parties: Power in an Emergent African Nation* (Princeton University Press 1963)

Peter Paret, *French Revolutionary Warfare from Indochina to Algeria: The Analysis of a Political and Military Doctrine* (Praeger 1964)

Harry Eckstein, ed., *Internal War: Problems and Approaches* (Free Press 1964)

Cyril E. Black and Thomas P. Thornton, eds., *Communism and Revolution: The Strategic Uses of Political Violence* (Princeton University Press 1964)

Miriam Camps, *Britain and the European Community 1955–1963* (Princeton University Press 1964)

Thomas P. Thornton, ed., *The Third World in Soviet Perspective: Studies by Soviet Writers on the Developing Areas* (Princeton University Press 1964)

James N. Rosenau, ed., *International Aspects of Civil Strife* (Princeton University Press 1964)

Sidney I. Ploss, *Conflict and Decision-Making in Soviet Russia: A Case Study of Agricultural Policy, 1953–1963* (Princeton University Press 1965)

Richard A. Falk and Richard J. Barnet, eds., *Security in Disarmament* (Princeton University Press 1965)

Karl von Vorys, *Political Development in Pakistan* (Princeton University Press 1965)

Harold and Margaret Sprout, *The Ecological Perspective on Human Affairs, With Special Reference to International Politics* (Princeton University Press 1965)

Klaus Knorr, *On the Uses of Military Power in the Nuclear Age* (Princeton University Press 1966)

Harry Eckstein, *Division and Cohesion in Democracy: A Study of Norway* (Princeton University Press 1966)

Cyril E. Black, *The Dynamics of Modernization: A Study in Comparative History* (Harper and Row 1966)

Peter Kunstadter, ed., *Southeast Asian Tribes, Minorities, and Nations* (Princeton University Press 1967)

E. Victor Wolfenstein, *The Revolutionary Personality: Lenin, Trotsky, Gandhi* (Princeton University Press 1967)

Leon Gordenker, *The UN Secretary-General and the Maintenance of Peace* (Columbia University Press 1967)

Oran R. Young, *The Intermediaries: Third Parties in International Crises* (Princeton University Press 1967)

James N. Rosenau, ed., *Domestic Sources of Foreign Policy* (Free Press 1967)

Richard F. Hamilton, *Affluence and the French Worker in the Fourth Republic* (Princeton University Press 1967)

Linda B. Miller, *World Order and Local Disorder: The United Nations and Internal Conflicts* (Princeton University Press 1967)

Wolfram F. Hanrieder, *West German Foreign Policy, 1949–1963: International Pressures and Domestic Response* (Stanford University Press 1967)

Richard H. Ullman, *Britain and the Russian Civil War: November 1918–February 1920* (Princeton University Press 1968)

Robert Gilpin, *France in the Age of the Scientific State* (Princeton University Press 1968)

William B. Bader, *The United States and the Spread of Nuclear Weapons* (Pegasus 1968)

Richard A. Falk, *Legal Order in a Violent World* (Princeton University Press 1968)

Cyril E. Black, Richard A. Falk, Klaus Knorr, and Oran R. Young, *Neutralization and World Politics* (Princeton University Press 1968)

Oran R. Young, *The Politics of Force: Bargaining During International Crises* (Princeton University Press 1969)

Klaus Knorr and James N. Rosenau, eds., *Contending Approaches to International Politics* (Princeton University Press 1969)

James N. Rosenau, ed., *Linkage Politics: Essays on the Convergence of National and International Systems* (Free Press 1969)

John T. McAlister, Jr., *Viet Nam: The Origins of Revolution* (Knopf 1969)

Jean Edward Smith, *Germany Beyond the Wall: People, Politics and Prosperity* (Little, Brown 1969)

James Barros, *Betrayal from Within: Joseph Avenol, Secretary-General of the League of Nations, 1933–1940* (Yale University Press 1969)

Charles Hermann, *Crises in Foreign Policy: A Simulation Analysis* (Bobbs-Merrill 1969)

Robert C. Tucker, *The Marxian Revolutionary Idea: Essays on Marxist Thought and Its Impact on Radical Movements* (W. W. Norton 1969)

Harvey Waterman, *Political Change in Contemporary France: The Politics of an Industrial Democracy* (Charles E. Merrill 1969)

Richard A. Falk and Cyril E. Black, eds., *The Future of the International Legal Order*, Vol. I, *Trends and Patterns* (Princeton University Press 1969)

Ted Robert Gurr, *Why Men Rebel* (Princeton University Press 1970)

C. S. Whitaker, Jr., *The Politics of Tradition: Continuity and Change in Northern Nigeria, 1946–1966* (Princeton University Press 1970)

Richard A. Falk, *The Status of Law in International Society* (Princeton University Press 1970)

Henry Bienen, *Tanzania: Party Transformation and Economic Development* (Princeton University Press 1967, rev. ed. 1970)

Klaus Knorr, *Military Power and Potential* (D. C. Heath 1970)

Richard A. Falk and Cyril E. Black, eds., *The Future of the International Legal Order*, Vol. II, *Wealth and Resources* (Princeton University Press 1970)

Leon Gordenker, ed., *The United Nations in International Politics* (Princeton University Press 1971)

Cyril E. Black and Richard A. Falk, eds., *The Future of the International Legal Order*, Vol. III, *Conflict Management* (Princeton University Press 1971)

Harold and Margaret Sprout, *Toward a Politics of the Planet Earth* (Van Nostrand Reinhold Co. 1971)

Francine R. Frankel, *India's Green Revolution: Economic Gains and Political Costs* (Princeton University Press 1971)

Cyril E. Black and Richard A. Falk, eds., *The Future of the International Legal Order*, Vol. IV, *The Structure of the International Environment* (Princeton University Press 1972)

Gerald Garvey, *Energy, Ecology, Economy* (W. W. Norton 1972)

Richard H. Ullman, *The Anglo-Soviet Accord* (Princeton University Press 1973)

Klaus Knorr, *Power and Wealth: The Political Economy of International Power* (Basic Books 1973)

OTHER BOOKS ON AFRICA WRITTEN
UNDER THE AUSPICES OF
HARVARD CENTER FOR INTERNATIONAL
AFFAIRS

Somali Nationalism, by Saadia Touval. Harvard University Press, 1963.

Africans on the Land, by Montague Yudelman. Harvard University Press, 1964.

The Rise of Nationalism in Central Africa, by Robert I. Rotberg. Harvard University Press, 1965.

Pan-Africanism and East African Integration, by Joseph S. Nye, Jr. Harvard University Press, 1965.

Political Change in a West African State, by Martin Kilson. Harvard University Press, 1966.

Planning without Facts: Lessons in Resource Allocation from Nigeria's Development, by Wolfgang F. Stolper. Harvard University Press, 1966.

Africa and United States Policy, by Rupert Emerson. Prentice-Hall, 1967.

Strike a Blow and Die: A Narrative of Race Relations in Colonial Africa, by George Simeon Mwase. Edited and introduced by Robert I. Rotberg. Harvard University Press, 1967; revised edition, 1970.

The Boundary Politics of Independent Africa, by Saadia Touval. Harvard University Press, 1972.

Library of Congress Cataloging in Publication Data

Bienen, Henry.
  Kenya: the politics of participation and control.

  "Written under the auspices of the Center of International
Studies, Princeton University, and the Center of International
Affairs, Harvard University."
  Bibliography: p.
  1. Political participation—Kenya. 2 Political parties—
Kenya. 3. Kenya—Economic policy. 4. policy. 4 Kenya—
Social conditions. I. Princeton University. Center of Inter-
national Studies. II. Harvard University. Center for Interna-
tional Affairs. III. Title.
JQ2947.A91B53   320.9′676′2   73-2461
ISBN 0-691-03096-0